SAS® Companion for the CMS Operating System, 1986 Edition

SAS Institute Inc.
SAS Circle □ Box 8000
Cary, NC 27512-8000

Marian Saffer wrote and **David D. Baggett** edited the *SAS® Companion for the CMS Operating System, 1986 Edition*.

The correct bibliographic citation for this manual is as follows: SAS Institute Inc. *SAS® Companion for the CMS Operating System, 1986 Edition*. Cary, NC: SAS Institute Inc., 1986. 102 pp.

SAS® Companion for the CMS Operating System, 1986 Edition

Copyright © 1986 by SAS Institute Inc., Cary, NC, USA.
ISBN 1-55544-001-0

90 89 4 3

Base SAS® software, the foundation of the SAS System, provides data retrieval and management, programming, statistical, and reporting capabilities. Also in the SAS System are SAS/GRAPH® SAS/FSP® SAS/ETS® SAS/IMS-DL/I® SAS/OR® SAS/AF® SAS/REPLAY-CICS® SAS/DMI® SAS/QC® SAS/SHARE® SAS/IML® SAS/STAT™ SAS/DB2™ SAS/SQL-DS™ SAS/CPE™ SAS/ASSIST™ and SAS/ACCESS™ software. Other products include SYSTEM 2000® Data Management Software, with basic SYSTEM 2000® QueX™ Multi-User™ CREATE™ Screen Writer™ and CICS interface software; SAS/RTERM® software; NeoVisuals™ software; and SAS/C® and SAS/CX™ compilers. *SAS Communications® SAS Training® SAS Views®* and SASware Ballot® are published by SAS Institute Inc. The Institute is a private company devoted to the support and further development of the software and related services.

Contents

Illustrations

Credits

The Version 5 CMS SAS software development team, directed by **Wayne F. Miller**, includes these people: **C. Michael Box**, **William L. Brideson**, **Keith V. Collins**, **Jenny A. Condrey**, **Timothy P. Hunter**, **Dennis E. Myers**, **Ronald O. Page**, **Maily T. Promislow**, **Sandra F. Tuning**, and **James C. Weathers III**.

CMS SAS software developers were responsible for the following procedures for Version 5:

PROC CONTENTS:	**Keith V. Collins**
PROC SORT:	**Timothy P. Hunter**
PROC TAPECOMP:	**Wayne F. Miller**
PROC TAPECOPY:	**Wayne F. Miller** and **James C. Weathers III**
PROC TAPELABEL:	**Wayne F. Miller** and **Timothy P. Hunter**

Technical Support for CMS SAS software is provided by **Gloria N. Cappy** and **Gwen G. Wiggs**.

Quality Assurance for CMS SAS software is performed by **Terry D. Poole**.

CMS SAS software testing at SAS Institute is carried out by **Gloria N. Cappy**, **Suzanne S. Gordon**, **Kenneth L. Holland**, **Sarah A. Howey**, **Harriet M. Janes**, Barbara A. Kennedy, **Ronald Parker**, **Terry D. Poole**, **Margaret A. Staab**, **Sharon M. Sanders**, and **Gwen G. Wiggs**.

Acknowledgments

The first implementation of SAS software under VM/CMS was by Romney White at the University of Waterloo. Since then, many users and installations have contributed to the development of the CMS SAS System with suggestions and assistance in testing the product. Special mention is due to:

Barbara Sakosky	Harvard University
Pat O'Meara	Adria Laboratories, Inc.
Ron Laing	Imperial Tobacco Ltd.
Louise Imbeau	Boeing Computer Services
Kent Kuiper	Boeing Computer Services
Mark Bugeaud	American Natural Resources
Arnie Kreuger	American Natural Resources
Jose Bauzo	Massachusetts Institute of Technology
Lois Kellerman	Massachusetts Institute of Technology
Bob Bolch	Texasgulf Inc.
Jim Gradolph	MortonNorwich, Inc.
Hubbard Helm	Rolscreen Company
Diane Reese	Metropolitan Washington Council of Governments
Ray Barnes	The Upjohn Company

The debugging tool DVS, written by Charlie Whitman, has saved us much time in problem solving.

The present version of this manual is based on the work of Virginia B. Sall, who wrote the first companion for the SAS System under CMS.

Preface

The *SAS Companion for the CMS Operating System, 1986 Edition* contains information specifically for SAS users working under the CMS operating system. This companion supplements documentation for base SAS software, the *SAS User's Guide: Basics, Version 5 Edition* and the *SAS User's Guide: Statistics, Version 5 Edition*.

What is the SAS System?

The SAS System is a software system for data analysis. The goal of SAS Institute is to provide one system that meets all computing needs. When your computing needs are met, you are free to concentrate on results rather than on the mechanics of getting them. Instead of learning programming languages, several statistical packages, and utility programs, you only need to learn the SAS System.

To the all-purpose base SAS software, you can add tools for graphics, forecasting, data entry, and interfaces to other data bases to provide one total system. The SAS System runs in batch and interactively under OS, TSO, CMS, VSE, SSX, and ICCF on IBM 370/30xx/43xx and compatible machines; on Digital Equipment Corporation's VAX™ 8xxx series and 11/7xx series under VMS™and on MicroVAX II™ under MicroVMS;™on Prime Computer Inc.'s Prime 50 series under PRIMOS,®on the IBM PC AT/370 and XT/370 under VM/PC; on Data General Corporation's ECLIPSE® MV series under AOS/VS; and on IBM PC XT and PC AT under PC DOS. To use any software product in the SAS System, you first need base SAS software. The PL/I Optimizing Transient Library is required for mainframe and VM/PC IBM systems. SYSTEM 2000 DBMS supports IBM 370/30xx/43xx and compatible machines under OS, TSO, CMS, DOS/VS(E), and CICS; the Sperry Series 1100 under OS 1100; and the Control Data 6000 and Cyber series under NOS and NOS/BE. Note: not all products are available for all operating systems.

Base SAS software provides tools for:

- information storage and retrieval
- data modification and programming
- report writing
- statistical analysis
- file handling.

Information storage and retrieval   The SAS System reads data values in virtually any form from cards, disk, tape, and your terminal screen; then it organizes the values into a SAS file. SAS files are stored in a directory; all SAS files in one directory belong to a SAS data library. The SAS System uses the SAS data library to give easy access to all SAS files in one directory.

Data modification and programming   A complete set of SAS statements and functions is available for modifying data. Some program statements perform standard operations such as creating new variables, accumulating totals, and checking for errors; others are powerful programming tools such as DO/END and IF-THEN/ELSE statements.

VAX and VMS are trademarks of Digital Equipment Corp., Maynard, MA, USA.

PRIMOS is the registered trademark of Prime Computer, Inc., Framingham, MA, USA.

ECLIPSE is the registered trademark of Data General Corp., Westboro, MA, USA.

Report writing Just as the SAS System reads data in almost any form, it can write data in almost any form. In addition to the preformatted reports that SAS procedures produce, SAS software users can design and produce printed reports in any form, as well as punched cards and output files.

Statistical analysis The statistical analysis procedures in the SAS System are among the finest available. They range from simple descriptive statistics to complex multivariate techniques. Their designs are based on our belief that you should never need to supply details that the SAS System can figure out. Statistical integrity is thus accompanied by ease of use. Especially noteworthy statistical features are the linear model procedures, of which GLM (General Linear Models) is the flagship.

File handling Combining values and observations from several data sets is often necessary for data analysis. SAS software has tools for editing, subsetting, concatenating, merging, and updating data sets. Multiple input files can be processed simultaneously, and several reports can be produced in one pass of the data.

Other SAS Software Products

With base SAS software, you can integrate SAS software products for graphics, data entry, operations research, and interfaces to other data bases to provide one total system:

- SAS/AF software—full-screen, interactive applications facility
- SAS/DMI software—an interface to the IBM facility ISPF that allows you to use the SAS language to write ISPF applications
- SAS/ETS software—expanded tools for business analysis, forecasting, and financial planning
- SAS/FSP software—interactive, menu-driven facilities for data entry, editing, retrieval of SAS files, letter writing, and spreadsheet analysis
- SAS/GRAPH software—device-intelligent color graphics for business and research applications
- SAS/IML software—multi-level, interactive programming language whose data elements are matrices
- SAS/IMS-DL/I software—interface for reading, updating, and writing IMS/VS or CICS DL/I data bases
- SAS/OR software—decision support tools for operations research and project management
- SAS/REPLAY-CICS software—interface that allows users of CICS/OS/VS and CICS/DOS/VS to store, manage, and replay SAS/GRAPH displays.

SAS Institute Documentation

Using this manual The companion can be used as a reference for experienced SAS users and as a learning tool for new users. The first chapter briefly defines the SAS System running under CMS and describes the organization of the rest of the book.

Subsequent chapters describe how to invoke the SAS System, create and read SAS files, and read and create external files. Handling of SAS standard output and work files is also discussed. Appendices describe storing user-written formats, how to transport SAS files to and from other operating systems, and other topics.

The companion supersedes the *SAS Companion for the VM/CMS Operating System, 1983 Edition*.

If you have any problems with this manual, please take time to complete the Your Turn page at the end of this book and send it to SAS Institute. We will consider your suggestions for future editions. In the meantime, ask your installation's SAS software consultant for help.

Other SAS Institute manuals and technical reports   Below is a list of user's guides for Version 5 of the SAS System:

SAS User's Guide: Basics, Version 5 Edition
SAS User's Guide: Statistics, Version 5 Edition
SAS/AF User's Guide, Version 5 Edition
SAS/ETS User's Guide, Version 5 Edition
SAS/FSP User's Guide, Version 5 Edition
SAS/GRAPH User's Guide, Version 5 Edition
SAS/GRAPH Guide to Hardware Interfaces, Version 5 Edition
SAS/IML User's Guide, Version 5 Edition
SAS/OR User's Guide, Version 5 Edition

Other manuals and technical reports of interest to CMS SAS users include:

SAS Programmer's Guide for PL/I, Version 5 Edition
SAS Guide to VSAM Processing, Version 5 Edition
"Downloading the VM/PC SAS System," SAS Technical Report P-140
"Guide to SAS/AF Menus, Version 5," SAS Technical Report P-141
"SAS/GRAPH Metagraphics Driver Facility: A Programmer's
    Guide," SAS Technical Report P-155

Write to SAS Institute for a current publications catalog, which describes the manuals as well as technical reports and lists their prices.

SAS Services to Users

Technical support   SAS Institute supports users through the Technical Support Department. If you have a problem running a SAS job, you should contact your site's SAS software representative. If the problem cannot be resolved locally, your local support personnel should call the Institute's Technical Support Department at (919) 467-8008 on weekdays between 9:00 a.m. and 8:00 p.m. Eastern Standard Time. A brochure describing the services provided by the Technical Support Department is available from SAS Institute.

Training   SAS Institute sponsors instructor-based, video-based, and computer-based training programs, including comprehensive courses of study for novice data processors, statisticians, applications programmers, systems programmers, and local support personnel. *SAS Training*, a semi-annual training publication, describes the total training program and each course currently being offered by SAS Institute.

News magazine   *SAS Communications* is the quarterly news magazine of SAS Institute. Each issue contains ideas for more effective use of the SAS System, information about research and development underway at SAS Institute, the current training schedule, new publications, and news of the SAS Users Group International (SUGI).

To receive a copy of *SAS Communications* regularly, send your name and complete address to:

SAS Institute Mailing List
SAS Institute Inc.
SAS Circle, Box 8000
Cary, NC 27512-8000

Sample library   The SAS Sample Library is included on the software installation tape and can be optionally installed at your site. The SAS Sample Library contains SAS applications to illustrate features of SAS procedures and creative SAS programming techniques that can help you gain an in-depth knowledge of SAS capabilities.

Here are a few examples of programs included:

ANOVA	analyzing a Latin-square split-plot design
ARIMA5	fitting an intervention model to an ozone time series
G3D2	three-dimensional plot of Iris species classification by physical measurement
IMLFFT	using the Finite Fourier Transform to compute a periodogram
CPM5A	summarizing resource utilization on a calendar
REG	modeling savings rates as a function of other population parameters
SPLINE	piece-wise regression analysis
VARCLUS	disjoint clustering variables.

Check with your SAS software representative to find out how to access the SAS Sample Library if it is available.

SUGI

The SAS Users Group International (SUGI) is a nonprofit association of professionals who are interested in how others are using the SAS System. Although SAS Institute provides administrative support, SUGI is independent from the Institute. Membership is open to all users at SAS sites, and there is no membership fee.

Annual conferences are structured to allow many avenues of discussion. Users present invited and contributed papers on various topics, for example:

- computer performance evaluation and systems software
- econometrics and time series
- graphics
- information systems
- interactive techniques
- statistics
- tutorials in SAS System software.

Proceedings of the annual conferences are distributed free to SUGI registrants. Extra copies may be purchased from SAS Institute. A SUGI registration package is sent to all users on the SAS Institute mailing list.

SASware Ballot   SAS users provide valuable input toward the direction of future SAS development by ranking their priorities on the annual SASware Ballot. The top vote-getters are announced at the SUGI conference. Complete results of the SASware Ballot are also printed in the *SUGI Proceedings*. The SASware Ballot is mailed to all users on the SAS Institute mailing list.

Supplemental library   SAS users at many installations have written their own SAS procedures for a wide variety of specialized applications. Some of these user-written procedures are available through the SUGI supplemental library and are documented in the *SUGI Supplemental Library User's Guide*. The procedures in the supplemental library are sent to each installation that licenses base SAS software, although only a few procedures are supported by SAS Institute staff.

Licensing the SAS System

The SAS System is licensed to customers in the Western Hemisphere from the Institute's headquarters in Cary, NC. To serve the needs of our international customers, the Institute maintains subsidiaries in the United Kingdom, New Zealand, Australia, Singapore, Germany, and France. In addition, agents in other countries are licensed distributors for the SAS System. For a complete list of offices, write or call:

SAS Institute Inc.
SAS Circle
Box 8000
Cary, NC 27512-8000
(919) 467-8000

Chapter 1

Introduction to the CMS SAS® System

WHAT IS THE CMS SAS SYSTEM?

SAS software runs under a variety of host operating systems, including VM/SP CMS. Generally speaking, SAS programs and their results are the same, regardless of the host operating system. For example, you use the same SAS statements to create a SAS data set and then print the data set under CMS as you would under any other operating system. However, the SAS System needs the host operating system's facilities for certain tasks, such as:

- making files available to a SAS program
- receiving input from and sending output to appropriate devices
- managing temporary and permanent memory in the computer
- supervisor services, including data and account security and routing of spool files.

Because each operating system handles such functions differently, the SAS System differs somewhat under each operating system. This book describes the use of base SAS software in a CMS environment.

WHAT THIS BOOK COVERS

The *SAS Companion for the CMS Operating System, 1986 Edition* describes how SAS behaves under CMS, for example, where output is routed after a program has executed, and how SAS accesses CMS files. This book also discusses how to use CMS and CP commands with SAS programs because using the CMS SAS System requires some interaction with CP (Control Program) and CMS (Conversational Monitor System) as well as interaction with SAS. You do not have to be a CMS expert to run CMS SAS programs; in fact, most of the time you need only a few CP and CMS commands. How much you need to know about CMS and CP depends upon how much you want CMS SAS to do for you.

You should not try to learn either SAS or CMS from this companion because it is not designed to be used alone. The companion is a supplement to other SAS documentation and IBM's CMS documentation. The **REFERENCES** section of this chapter contains a list of important reference manuals for the SAS System and CMS.

As you read this companion or any SAS or IBM manual, remember that your computer installation may have modified SAS and/or CMS to suit the needs of your local computing environment. The SAS software consultant at your site should be able to provide information on any modifications that affect CMS SAS programs.

Organization

The *SAS Companion for the CMS Operating System, 1986 Edition* was written for a wide range of SAS users. You will probably find that some sections contain information on features you do not use. Feel free to skip sections that do not apply to your use of CMS SAS; for example, if you never use tapes, skip discussions of SAS files and external files on tape.

The following descriptions of the contents of each chapter in the companion can help you decide which chapters are applicable to your use of the CMS SAS System.

Chapter 2, "SAS Programs under CMS," discusses how SAS is invoked and the modes of execution under CMS. Interactive and noninteractive SAS programs, and ways of issuing CMS and CP commands from within a SAS program are described.

Chapter 3, "Output and WORK Files," describes utility files that are used in CMS SAS programs. Files referenced in Chapter 2, such as the SAS log file, are discussed in more detail.

Chapter 4, "CMS SAS Files," begins with descriptions of the kinds of SAS files and how to name a SAS file. Then creating and using permanent SAS files are discussed, with separate sections for disk-format and tape-format SAS files.

Chapter 5, "Using External Files in CMS SAS Programs," provides information on creating and accessing non-SAS files in CMS SAS. Again, disk files and tape files are described separately.

Chapter 6, "SAS System Options," tells you how to override SAS system option default settings and describes SAS system options used only for CMS SAS programs.

Chapter 7, "Memory and Space Requirements," provides general guidelines for the amount of memory needed for CMS SAS programs. The chapter also recommends solutions for problems caused by insufficient memory and space.

This book includes five appendices:

- Appendix 1 is a glossary of terms used in the companion. Refer to this appendix when you encounter unfamiliar terminology in your reading.
- Appendix 2 is about storing user-written formats created by PROC FORMAT.
- Appendix 3 discusses cross-system compatibility and CMS SAS files, and the access of AOS/VS, OS, PRIMOS, VM/PC, VMS, and VSE SAS files from CMS SAS.
- Appendix 4 provides an example of the use of a CMS EXEC in a SAS application and describes two SAS features you can use with EXECs: the GETEXEC function and the PUTEXEC CALL routine.
- Appendix 5 describes PROC TAPECOMP, a SAS procedure for comparing files on two tapes.

New SAS Users

If you have not used the SAS System before, you can get started by following the examples in this book. However, you also need to read some background material on SAS to understand what the examples are doing. The *SAS Introductory Guide* provides a quick overview of SAS and its capabilities and gives sufficient information to write many SAS programs. You should also have access to the *SAS User's Guide: Basics, Version 5 Edition* and the *SAS User's Guide: Statistics, Version 5 Edition* for a complete discussion of base SAS software. These books are the primary documentation on the use and syntax of SAS statements, options, and procedures. You do not need to read all of this material to begin using SAS; read the *Introductory Guide* and run the examples in this companion while you familiarize yourself with the basic SAS concepts. Consult additional documentation as questions occur to you.

Check with your SAS software consultant about any modifications your computer installation may have made to SAS or CMS that cause them to behave differently from the way they are documented in this book.

New CMS Users

If you are a new CMS user, you should have access to IBM's *CMS Primer* or the *CMS Primer for Line-Oriented Terminals*, depending on the kind of terminal you use. These books introduce you to the basic concepts, commands, and features of CMS. You should also have access to the *CMS User's Guide* and the *CMS Command and Macro Reference*. See the **REFERENCES** section at the end of this chapter for more CMS titles and order numbers.

Many examples of SAS programs in the following chapters use one or more CP and CMS commands. You need to learn a number of these commands to use SAS and CMS effectively, but you do not need to become a CMS expert to proceed. Begin doing the examples, and look up the CP and CMS commands as you use them. Refer to IBM's documentation as questions occur to you.

Your computer installation may have made alterations to CMS so that some features behave differently from the way they are documented by IBM or in this book. Computer installation personnel can provide information on local modifications to CMS.

NOTATION AND TERMINOLOGY CONVENTIONS

When SAS features, function keys, statements, options, and procedures are discussed in this book, the assumption is that default conditions are in effect unless otherwise stated. Your SAS environment and SAS programs may be different because you (or your installation) have altered defaults.

The examples using screens and sample terminal sessions in this book may look slightly different from your own terminal sessions, depending on your CMS installation. The environment used for the examples in this book is outlined below.

- In general, information that you enter appears in lowercase, and SAS and CMS responses are in uppercase. Exceptions: model SAS statements or CMS and CP commands used for illustration within text are shown in uppercase. Also, when information is actually stored in lowercase or mixed upper- and lowercase, CMS displays the data in upper- and lowercase.

- By default, SAS prompts for input with one of these:

      n?
      n>

  where *n* is a line number of a SAS statement or data line.
- The examples in this book were done on a full-screen IBM PC XT/370 used as a CMS terminal. The short form of the CMS prompt (ready message) is used:

      R;

  Prompt characters vary from CMS installation to installation.

SAMPLE DATA SET

Most of the examples in this book are based on a sample of data from a fictional study of the effects of different doses of a drug. Each subject in the study receives a particular dose of the experimental drug, and then the rate of decrease in a certain bacteria is measured. Subject weight and age information are included. The data are in a SAS data set called DRUG432.MONITOR (CMS file MONITOR DRUG432). The variables in the data set and their attributes are shown in **Table 1.1**.

Table 1.1   Variables in the Sample Data Set DRUG432.MONITOR

SAS Variable	Type	Informat	Format
SUBJECT	character	$7.	
WEIGHT	numeric	3.	
AGE	numeric	2.	
DOSEDATE	numeric	DATE7.	DATE7.
DOSE	numeric	3.	
INITBAC	numeric	2.	
BACCNT	numeric	2.	
CHCKDATE	numeric	DATE7.	DATE7.

The SAS DATA step used to create the sample data set is shown below:

```
CMS FILEDEF DOSEDATA DISK DRUG DOSES A;
DATA DRUG432.MONITOR;
   INFILE DOSEDATA;
   INPUT a1 SUBJECT $7. a9 WEIGHT 3. a13 AGE 2.
         a16 DOSEDATE DATE7. a24 DOSE 3. a28 INITBAC 2.
         a31 CHCKDATE DATE7. a39 BACCNT 2.;
   FORMAT DOSEDATE CHCKDATE DATE7.;
RUN;
```

REFERENCES

International Business Machines Corporation, *Virtual Machine/System Product: CMS Command and Macro Reference*, SC19-6209.

International Business Machines Corporation, *IBM Virtual Machine/System Product: CMS Primer*, SC24-5236.

International Business Machines Corporation, *IBM Virtual Machine/System Product: CMS Primer for Line-Oriented Terminals*, SC24-5236.

International Business Machines Corporation, *IBM Virtual Machine/System Product: CMS User's Guide*, SC19-6210.

International Business Machines Corporation, *IBM Virtual Machine/System Product: CP Command Reference for General Users*, SC19-6211.

International Business Machines Corporation, *IBM Virtual Machine/System Product: Introduction*, GC19-6200.

International Business Machines Corporation, *IBM Virtual Machine/System Product: System Messages and Codes*, SC19-6204.

International Business Machines Corporation, *IBM Virtual Machine/System Product: System Product Interpreter User's Guide*, SC24-5238.

International Business Machines Corporation, *IBM Virtual Machine/System Product: System Product Interpreter Reference Guide*, SC24-5239.

International Business Machines Corporation, *IBM Virtual Machine/System Product System Product Editor Command and Macro Reference*, SC24-5221.

International Business Machines Corporation, *IBM Virtual Machine/System Product System Product Editor User's Guide*, SC24-5220.

SAS Institute Inc. (1985), *SAS Guide to VSAM Processing*, Cary, NC, SAS Institute Inc.

SAS Institute Inc. (1985), *SAS Introductory Guide*, Cary, NC, SAS Institute Inc.

SAS Institute Inc. (1985), *SAS User's Guide: Basics, Version 5 Edition*, Cary, NC, SAS Institute Inc.

SAS Institute Inc. (1985), *SAS User's Guide: Statistics, Version 5 Edition*, Cary, NC, SAS Institute Inc.

SAS® Programs
under CMS

INTRODUCTION

This chapter discusses the CMS SAS interface, the modes of SAS execution under CMS, interrupting SAS sessions, and using CMS and CP commands in a SAS session.

Many SAS statements and options and CMS and CP commands are mentioned in this chapter. Consult the references listed at the end of Chapter 1 for complete descriptions of statements, options, and commands.

THE CMS SAS SYSTEM INTERFACE

The SAS System is adapted to run under CMS by the CMS SAS interface. When you invoke the SAS System, the interface:

- automatically issues CMS FILEDEFs for required SAS files
- constructs a list of text libraries to be searched during the SAS session and issues GLOBAL commands for those libraries.

During a SAS session, the interface:

- handles memory and I/O management
- can invoke CMS and CP commands specified in the SAS source statements
- can get SAS source statements from CMS files by issuing FILEDEFs automatically.

At the end of a SAS session, the interface:

- erases temporary SAS files and work files
- closes any files that are still open
- restores the list of GLOBALed text libraries to its status before invoking SAS
- clears FILEDEFs issued by SAS.

MODES OF EXECUTION

There are several different ways of submitting a program for execution. These methods are often referred to as *modes of execution* or *execution modes*.

As a CMS user, you may be familiar with execution modes called *interactive processing* and *batch processing*:

- Interactive processing under CMS means that the work you are doing and the programs you are running are executing in your virtual machine. Your terminal is *dedicated* to the programs you execute or the applications you are running. This is sometimes called *conversational mode*.
- Batch processing under CMS means that you submit a program for execution to a special CMS userid rather than executing it under your userid in your own virtual machine. The special userid is for the *batch machine*, which is controlled by the system operator. Programs submitted for batch processing are *spooled* to the batch machine userid, where they are executed in sequence. Batch processing is useful when you need to run programs that take a long time to execute because it leaves your terminal free for other applications (in interactive mode).

Any SAS program you execute under CMS is run under one of these two basic CMS execution modes. However, the SAS System offers three variations of execution under CMS's interactive mode, as well as batch SAS program execution. Therefore, there are four possible modes of execution for SAS programs. These are depicted in **Figure 2.1** and described briefly below.

1. In CMS interactive mode you can execute an *interactive SAS display manager session*. The SAS Display Manager System is a full-screen facility. It allows you to enter SAS programming statements on one screen (the program editor screen), execute them with a SUBMIT command, and view the log and procedure output on two other screens (the log and output screens). This execution mode is very convenient for users with full-screen terminals.

2. In CMS interactive mode you can also execute an *interactive SAS line-prompt session*, also called a *line-mode session*. In line-prompt mode, SAS prompts you to enter SAS statements at the terminal, one line at a time. After you have entered a DATA or PROC step, SAS executes the statements in that step and displays the results on your screen. This mode is convenient for many applications on a line-mode terminal.

3. The third kind of SAS execution under CMS interactive mode is called *noninteractive*. To use noninteractive mode, you must first store a SAS program in a CMS file. Then to run the program, you invoke SAS, specifying the filename of the file containing the SAS statements. Although this executes under interactive CMS, it is called noninteractive because the program runs with no intervention from the terminal. Noninteractive execution is useful for running programs repeatedly or running programs once they have been perfected.

4. Finally, you can run SAS programs in *batch mode* by submitting them to a CMS batch machine rather than executing them on your own virtual machine. CMS batch machines are used if a program requires a long time to run or if a terminal is unavailable. CMS SAS programs run in a batch machine do not differ in content from noninteractive or interactive programs you run in your own virtual machine. However, this is called batch mode because your terminal is not dedicated to the SAS program while it executes, so you are free to perform other tasks.

Each of the four SAS execution modes is discussed in separate sections later in this chapter.

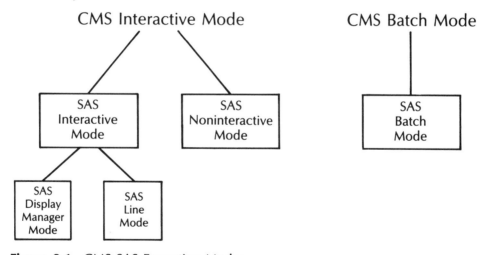

Figure 2.1 CMS SAS Execution Modes

THE SAS COMMAND

Regardless of the execution mode you use, you always begin a SAS session or program by making a request to CMS to use the SAS System. You make your request to CMS with the *SAS command*. Note that the SAS command is a CMS EXEC written by SAS Institute; it is not documented in IBM's manuals on CMS.

The form of the SAS command is

SAS *filename ... (options*

The italicized specifications, which are described below, are optional. The specifications you use determine the mode of execution.

filename   identifies a CMS file containing SAS statements. Specifying a filename on the SAS command invokes a noninteractive SAS session. Omit the filename to begin an interactive SAS display manager or line-prompt session.

A file specified on the SAS command must have filetype SAS, but it can reside on any accessed disk. Files of SAS statements must contain fixed-length, 80-character records.

You can specify as many as twelve filenames on the SAS command. The files are processed in the order in which they are listed.

options   allows you to specify many SAS system options. You must precede options with a left parenthesis on the SAS command. **Do not use an equals sign for value options specified on the SAS command.**

If you do not specify a filename on the SAS command **and** you are using a full-screen terminal, a display manager session begins by default. You must have NODMS in effect to use line-mode on a full-screen terminal.

Below are some examples of SAS commands.

- To invoke an interactive SAS session, without specifying any SAS system options, enter:

    ```
    SAS
    ```

- To invoke an interactive SAS session and specify some SAS system options, for example NODATE and USER, enter:

    ```
    SAS (NODATE USER DRUG432
    ```

- To invoke an interactive SAS line-prompt session from a full-screen terminal, specifying the NODMS SAS system option to override display manager, enter:

    ```
    SAS (NODMS
    ```

- To invoke a noninteractive SAS program (without specifying SAS system options), where REPORT SAS is the file containing the SAS programming statements, enter:

    ```
    SAS REPORT
    ```

- To invoke the same noninteractive SAS program and specify some SAS system options, enter:

    ```
    SAS REPORT (NODATE USER DRUG432
    ```

INTERACTIVE DISPLAY MANAGER EXECUTION MODE

If you use a full-screen terminal, you can use display manager for interactive SAS sessions. Display manager is a versatile and convenient facility for SAS programming. The program editor screen has built-in, full-screen editing, making it easy to write SAS programs and to submit them for execution. Output can be reviewed immediately in the log and output screens. The facility supports use of your terminal's function keys, including scrolling and split-screen capabilities. You can direct both SAS programs and SAS output to disk files even after they are displayed on the screen, and you can call external files containing SAS programs in order to execute them from the program editor screen.

Display manager is described in the *SAS User's Guide: Basics, Version 5 Edition* and in each SAS software product user's guide. You should refer to one of these documents for the primary description of display manager. The list below points out some of display manager's features.

- The **program editor screen** is available for inputting and editing SAS program statements. In addition to editing features, a variety of special display manager commands can be used to perform functions such as submitting SAS programs, saving programs in disk files, recalling previously executed SAS steps, calling SAS programs stored in external files, scrolling, and setting editing environment features like line size and line numbering.
- The **log screen** and the **output screen** allow you to browse the output from programs executed from the program editor screen. These two screens support commands for scrolling through output, saving output in disk files, and establishing the browsing environment.
- Special **command-line commands**, designed especially for display manager, allow you to submit programs, create and save disk files, call in external files, and perform many other functions from the command line of any screen.
- In the program editor screen you can use **line commands** to make editing easier. You can specify many line commands on both single lines and blocks of lines. Examples of line commands are those for moving lines, copying lines, splitting lines, and deleting lines.
- You can **reformat display manager screens** by splitting the terminal screen where you like and using color and highlighting attributes.
- There is a set of **function keys**, including some that are short-cut methods of executing display manager commands. To check function key settings or to change settings, use the KEYS command-line command.
- You use **editing keys** in the program editor screen for a number of routine editing functions, like deleting characters, inserting characters, moving to a new line, and so on.

Note: the many powerful features of display manager demand a larger virtual machine. When executing SAS programs in interactive display manager mode, you need to allow 600K of memory for display manager (in addition to memory required for other SAS processing).

A Sample Display Manager Session

Screens 2.1 through **2.7** show a sample SAS program executed in interactive display manager mode. Defaults are assumed for all features. Follow the explanation of the sample session by matching the circled numbers in the screens to the items in the numbered list below.

Screen 2.1 shows what your terminal screen looks like when an interactive display manager session is invoked with this SAS command:

SAS

1. The program editor screen is at the bottom of your terminal screen initially. The line labeled "Command ===>" and the numbered lines are *unprotected fields*, that is, fields in which you can enter or alter information. Enter command-line commands in the Command ===>

field. Enter the SAS programming statements you want to execute in the fields after the line numbers. Although eight or fewer text fields are displayed initially, you can have as many lines of SAS code as you like by scrolling and adding more lines. Also, you can display more than eight lines of the program editor screen by using the SPLIT function key or the SPLIT command.

2. Initially, the log screen is at the top of the terminal screen. The line labeled "Command ===>" is the only unprotected field of the log screen. Use the Command ===> field to enter valid display manager command-line commands. The remainder of the log screen is where the SAS log is displayed after you execute SAS programming statements from the program editor.

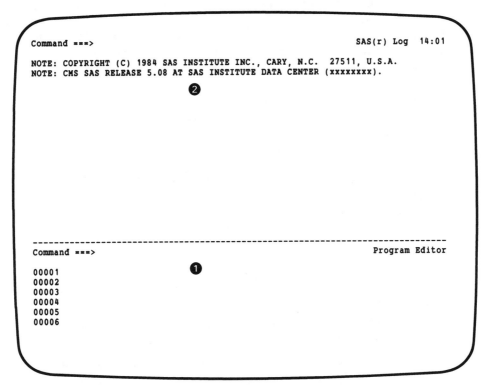

```
Command ===>                                            SAS(r) Log  14:01

NOTE: COPYRIGHT (C) 1984 SAS INSTITUTE INC., CARY, N.C.  27511, U.S.A.
NOTE: CMS SAS RELEASE 5.08 AT SAS INSTITUTE DATA CENTER (xxxxxxxx).
                                   ❷




_____
Command ===>                                            Program Editor
00001                              ❶
00002
00003
00004
00005
00006
```

Screen 2.1   Initial Display Manager Screens

Screen 2.2 shows the program editor and log screens with a SAS DATA step typed in but not yet submitted for execution. **Screen 2.3** shows how the log and program editor screens look after the sample program is executed with the SUBMIT command-line command.

3. The log screen displays the SAS log from the DATA step. You can scroll forward and backward through the log information with the FORWARD and BACKWARD function keys (keys 7 and 8).

4. The program editor screen is now blank because the code entered there earlier has been executed.

```
Command ===>                                          SAS(r) Log  14:01

NOTE: COPYRIGHT (C) 1984 SAS INSTITUTE INC., CARY, N.C.  27511, U.S.A.
NOTE: CMS SAS RELEASE 5.08 AT SAS INSTITUTE DATA CENTER (xxxxxxxx).








-----------------------------------------------------------------------
Command ===> submit                                      Program Editor

00001 data dose200;
00002    set drug432.monitor;
00003      if dose=200;
00004 run;
00005
00006
```

Screen 2.2   Program Editor and Log Screens before Executing Program

```
Command ===>                                          SAS(r) Log  14:02

NOTE: COPYRIGHT (C) 1984 SAS INSTITUTE INC., CARY, N.C.  27511, U.S.A.
NOTE: CMS SAS RELEASE 5.08 AT SAS INSTITUTE DATA CENTER (xxxxxxxx).

  1 data dose200;                          ❸
  2    set drug432.monitor;
  3      if dose=200;
  4 run;
NOTE: DATA SET WORK.DOSE200 HAS 40 OBSERVATIONS AND 8 VARIABLES.





-----------------------------------------------------------------------
Command ===>                                             Program Editor

00001                          ❹
00002
00003
00004
00005
00006
```

Screen 2.3   Program Editor and Log Screens after Executing Program

To see the display manager's output screen, we execute a PROC PRINT step. The PROC PRINT step is shown in **Screen 2.4** before execution.

```
Command ===>                                          SAS(r) Log   14:02

  NOTE: COPYRIGHT (C) 1984 SAS INSTITUTE INC., CARY, N.C.  27511, U.S.A.
  NOTE: CMS SAS RELEASE 5.08 AT SAS INSTITUTE DATA CENTER (xxxxxxxx).

   1 data dose200;                        ❺
   2    set drug432.monitor;
   3    if dose=200;
   4 run;
  NOTE: DATA SET WORK.DOSE200 HAS 40 OBSERVATIONS AND 8 VARIABLES.




  ----------------------------------------------------------------------
  Command ===> submit                                      Program Editor

  00001 proc print data=dose200;     ❻
  00002    var subject weight age baccnt chckdate;
  00003 run;
  00004
  00005
  00006
```

Screen 2.4   Display before Executing Another Program

5. The SAS log from the previously executed DATA step is still displayed.
6. The PROC step statements are added in the program editor screen, and the SUBMIT command is entered on the command line.

Screen 2.5 shows the output screen, which is displayed automatically after a PROC step executes successfully.

7. The first page of procedure output is displayed. You can scroll forward and backward through the output using the FORWARD and BACKWARD function keys. By default, there is no command line on the output screen. To add a command line so that you can execute commands from the output screen, use the function key assigned to the COMMAND command (function key 2).
8. **Screen 2.6** shows the output screen with a command line added.

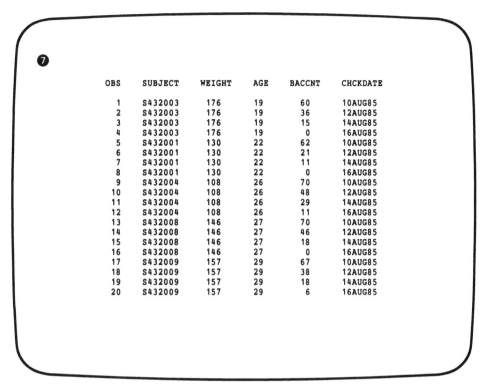

Screen 2.5   Default Output Screen

```
Command ===>                                              Procedure Output
    8

        OBS    SUBJECT   WEIGHT   AGE   BACCNT   CHCKDATE

         1     S432003     176     19      60     10AUG85
         2     S432003     176     19      36     12AUG85
         3     S432003     176     19      15     14AUG85
         4     S432003     176     19       0     16AUG85
         5     S432001     130     22      62     10AUG85
         6     S432001     130     22      21     12AUG85
         7     S432001     130     22      11     14AUG85
         8     S432001     130     22       0     16AUG85
         9     S432004     108     26      70     10AUG85
        10     S432004     108     26      48     12AUG85
        11     S432004     108     26      29     14AUG85
        12     S432004     108     26      11     16AUG85
        13     S432008     146     27      70     10AUG85
        14     S432008     146     27      46     12AUG85
        15     S432008     146     27      18     14AUG85
        16     S432008     146     27       0     16AUG85
        17     S432009     157     29      67     10AUG85
        18     S432009     157     29      38     12AUG85
```

Screen 2.6   Output Screen with Command Line Added

To return to the program editor and log screens from the output screen, use the END function key (function key 3). When you return to the program editor and log screens, the display is as shown in **Screen 2.7**.

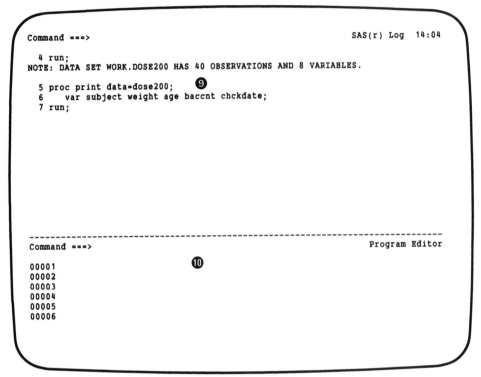

```
Command ===>                                      SAS(r) Log   14:04

   4 run;
NOTE: DATA SET WORK.DOSE200 HAS 40 OBSERVATIONS AND 8 VARIABLES.

   5 proc print data=dose200;     ➒
   6    var subject weight age baccnt chckdate;
   7 run;







----------------------------------------------------------------------
Command ===>                                      Program Editor

00001                        ➓
00002
00003
00004
00005
00006
```

Screen 2.7   Program Editor and Log Screens after PROC Step

9. The log screen displays the log entries from the PROC step just executed, as well as information from the earlier DATA step.
10. The program editor screen is blank because the code has executed.

To exit the SAS display manager session, execute an ENDSAS statement from the program editor screen or a BYE command from the command line of any display manager screen.

Recalling SAS Programs

One of the display manager command-line commands is RECALL. When the RECALL command executes, it retrieves and displays in the program editor screen the last set of SAS statements executed. By repeatedly issuing RECALL commands, you can redisplay all of the previously executed programs from your session. By default, the RECALL command is assigned to function key 4.

RECALL makes it easy to correct errors in your SAS programs. When you execute a program containing mistakes, the log displayed in the log screen includes ERROR messages and warning NOTEs. You can RECALL the SAS code that produced the errors, make corrections based on log information with the program editor, and resubmit the program.

INTERACTIVE LINE-MODE EXECUTION

If you do not have a full-screen terminal, you can use line-mode sessions for interactive execution. Users with full-screen terminals can also run line-mode sessions by specifying NODMS on the SAS command.

In an interactive line-mode session, SAS prompts you for input lines, one at a time. When you have entered a complete SAS step or steps, enter a RUN statement to execute the step. The SAS log information and the procedure output are displayed on the terminal screen automatically. Then you can continue with more SAS steps, as needed.

Sample Line-Mode Session

Screen 2.8 shows a sample SAS line-mode session. Follow the explanation of the example by matching the numbered comments below with the corresponding circled numbers in the screen.

1. When CMS prompts, enter the SAS command to start the SAS line-mode session. Note that you must specify the NODMS option on the SAS command **if you are using a full-screen terminal** because display manager is the default for interactive execution on full-screen devices. If your terminal is not a full-screen terminal, NODMS can be omitted. The NOSOURCE system option is specified to prevent each input line from being echoed.
2. SAS responds with a message noting the release of SAS being used, 5.08 in this case, and the SAS installation name and site number.
3. Now SAS prompts you to enter SAS statements. Each prompt consists of a line number followed by a question mark and perhaps a prompt character (such as >) determined by your CMS installation. Type in SAS statements in response to these line number prompts, pressing the ENTER key when you have finished a line.
4. Execute the step by entering the RUN statement. (Note that PROC OPTIONS executes immediately, without a RUN statement.)

   Alternatively, you can omit the RUN statement at the end of a step, and SAS executes the step when another DATA or PROC statement is encountered. However, this causes processing notes and output pertaining to the executing step to be typed in the middle of the SAS statements for the new step. If you use the RUN statement, SAS output is easier to read because it is displayed before you begin entering the next SAS step.
5. Now the current step is executed. By default, SAS types any processing notes and procedure output at the terminal.
6. After the current step has executed and its output is displayed, SAS prompts you for another SAS statement. Continue the SAS session with another DATA or PROC step, or terminate the SAS session by entering the ENDSAS statement or a /* in columns 1 and 2 of a line.

```
R;
sas (nodms nosource          ❶
NOTE: COPYRIGHT (C) 1984 SAS INSTITUTE INC., CARY, N.C.   27511, U.S.A.
NOTE: CMS SAS RELEASE 5.08 AT SAS INSTITUTE DATA CENTER (xxxxxxxx).      ❷

  1?      ❸
data dose200;
  2?
   set drug432.monitor;
  3?
   if dose=200;
  4?
run;      ❹
NOTE: DATA SET WORK.DOSE200 HAS 40 OBSERVATIONS AND 8 VARIABLES.      ❺

  5?      ❻
proc print data=dose200;
  6>
   var subject weight age baccnt chckdate;
  7>
run;
              OBS     SUBJECT     WEIGHT    AGE    BACCNT    CHCKDATE

                1     S432003      176      19       60      10AUG85
                2     S432003      176      19       36      12AUG85
                3     S432003      176      19       15      14AUG85
                4     S432003      176      19        0      16AUG85
                5     S432001      130      22       62      10AUG85
                6     S432001      130      22       21      12AUG85
                7     S432001      130      22       11      14AUG85
                8     S432001      130      22        0      16AUG85
                9     S432004      108      26       70      10AUG85
               10     S432004      108      26       48      12AUG85
               11     S432004      108      26       29      14AUG85
               12     S432004      108      26       11      16AUG85
               13     S432008      146      27       70      10AUG85
               14     S432008      146      27       46      12AUG85
               15     S432008      146      27       18      14AUG85
               16     S432008      146      27        0      16AUG85
               17     S432009      157      29       67      10AUG85
               18     S432009      157      29       38      12AUG85
               19     S432009      157      29       18      14AUG85
               20     S432009      157      29        6      16AUG85

              OBS     SUBJECT     WEIGHT    AGE    BACCNT    CHCKDATE

               21     S432007      165      30       65      10AUG85
               22     S432007      165      30       43      12AUG85
               23     S432007      165      30       18      14AUG85
               24     S432007      165      30        8      16AUG85
               25     S432002      195      35       45      10AUG85
               26     S432002      195      35       18      12AUG85
               27     S432002      195      35        9      14AUG85
               28     S432002      195      35        0      16AUG85
               29     S432006      140      36       54      10AUG85
               30     S432006      140      36       28      12AUG85
               31     S432006      140      36       11      14AUG85
               32     S432006      140      36        0      16AUG85
               33     s432010      164      43       60      10AUG85
               34     s432010      164      43       38      12AUG85
               35     s432010      164      43       20      14AUG85
               36     s432010      164      43        8      16AUG85
               37     S432005      137      58       64      10AUG85
               38     S432005      137      58       42      12AUG85
               39     S432005      137      58       19      14AUG85
               40     S432005      137      58        3      16AUG85

  8?
```

Screen 2.8 Sample Line-Mode Session Input Lines and Output

What If You Make a Mistake?

The preceding example was a perfect session with no typing errors, but most people make some typing or syntax errors during a session. If you are using a full-screen terminal, you can correct mistakes caught in the middle of a line (before you press ENTER) with cursor movements.

If you use a line-mode terminal and notice an error before you have completely entered a line, you can make the correction with the CMS logical line-editing symbols. For example, if you are typing a DATA statement, but type DSTS rather than DATA, and an at sign (@) is the character-delete symbol, you can correct the line like this:

```
DSTS@@@ATA COUNTS;
```

If you enter a SAS statement with a syntax error, the SAS System issues an ERROR message in the middle of the DATA or PROC step. (SAS underlines the part of the statement it does not understand and prints an error number and the explanation associated with the error.) If you get an ERROR message in the middle of a step, enter a RUN statement to clear out the current step. Then repeat the statements for the step in which the error occurred. See **Screen 2.9** for an example of this situation.

```
   8?
data dose250;
   9?
    set drug432.monitor;
  10?
    if dose 250;
  10     if dose 250;
                ----
                301
                  309
ERROR 301: INVALID SYNTAX, OR MISSING INFIX OPERATOR, ';', ',', OR ')'.
ERROR 309: THE EXPRESSION IS INCOMPLETE.
  11?
run;
NOTE: SAS STOPPED PROCESSING THIS STEP BECAUSE OF ERRORS.
NOTE: DATA SET WORK.DOSE250 HAS 0 OBSERVATIONS AND 8 VARIABLES.

  12?
data dose250;
  13?
    set drug432.monitor;
  14?
    if dose=250;
  15?
run;
NOTE: DATA SET WORK.DOSE250 HAS 40 OBSERVATIONS AND 8 VARIABLES.
```

Screen 2.9   Using the RUN Statement to End a Problem Step

Note: if the SAS system option SPOOL is in effect, you can use the %LIST statement to view lines already entered and the %INCLUDE statement to repeat correctly entered lines. See the discussion of %INCLUDE later in this chapter.

Some mistakes cause the SAS System to issue NOTEs and warnings in the middle of a step but do not cause an error condition or an ERROR message. For example, SAS issues a NOTE when you enter a variable value that conflicts with the variable's type (character or numeric). If no ERROR message is issued, you can continue to input the step and execute it.

For more discussion on diagnosing errors in SAS programs, see the *SAS Applications Guide*.

Saving SAS Statements

You can save statements entered during a line-mode session in a CMS file by specifying the TLOG system option on the SAS command:

```
SAS (NODMS TLOG
```

Specifying TLOG causes the lines you enter during a SAS session to be saved in a CMS file on your A-disk. The filetype is always SAS. The filename is either one you specify with the NAME option or SAS if you do not specify the NAME option. The only lines written to the TLOG file are statements that you enter; responses from the system do not appear.*

NONINTERACTIVE EXECUTION MODE

When SAS programs are stored in CMS files, the SAS session can be conducted without your intervention. To invoke SAS for noninteractive execution, specify a CMS file containing SAS statements on the SAS command:

SAS *filename ...(options*

You can specify a single filename or a list of up to twelve filenames in the order they are to be processed. You can specify SAS system options after a left parenthesis, as usual.

A file of SAS statements can be constructed by

- a CMS editor
- another program
- the SAVE command in a display manager session
- using the TLOG option in a line-mode SAS session.

To use a CMS file of SAS statements for noninteractive execution, the file **must** have filetype SAS, but it can reside on any accessed disk. The file must contain fixed-length, 80-character lines. (By default, all 80 characters of the source lines are scanned. Use the SAS system option S= to limit the number of columns scanned.)

For example, suppose you used a CMS editor to create a file containing a SAS program that produces plots of a SAS data set. The file's file-id is PLOTDOSE SAS A, and it contains this SAS program:

```
PROC PLOT DATA=DRUG432.MONITOR UNIFORM;
   BY DOSE;
   PLOT BACCNT*WEIGHT / VAXIS=0 TO 80 BY 2 HAXIS=100 TO 200 BY 10;
   PLOT BACCNT*CHCKDATE / VAXIS=0 TO 80 BY 2;
RUN;
```

Use this SAS command to execute the program:

```
SAS PLOTDOSE
```

When you execute a SAS program noninteractively, the log and procedure output do not appear on your screen automatically. Instead, output is written to two

---

* A /* entered to terminate a SAS session does not appear in such a file.

CMS files on your A-disk: one for the SAS log and one for the procedure output. The filetype of the file containing the SAS log is always SASLOG. The filetype of the file containing procedure output (if any) is always LISTING.

The SASLOG and LISTING files are assigned the same filename. The filename is determined by the NAME option or, if you do not specify the NAME option, by the filename of the first SAS source file mentioned on the SAS command. For the PLOTDOSE example, two files are created: PLOTDOSE SASLOG A, which contains the SAS log, and PLOTDOSE LISTING A, which contains the output from the PLOT procedure.

Like any CMS file, SASLOG and LISTING files from noninteractive SAS programs can be displayed at the terminal with the CMS TYPE command, printed with the CMS PRINT command, or viewed with an editor.

When you use the TYPE command,

- the carriage-control characters in column 1 of each line of a SASLOG file are displayed. The TYPE command does not automatically drop carriage-control characters in a SASLOG file, so they appear on the screen unless you use the CMS option COL to skip column 1. For example, to list PLOTDOSE SASLOG A without carriage-control characters, use this TYPE command:

```
TYPE PLOTDOSE SASLOG A (COL 2
```

- the carriage-control characters in column 1 of the lines of a LISTING file are dropped automatically. Therefore, the COL option is not needed in the TYPE command for a LISTING file.

In **Screen 2.10**, the TYPE command is invoked to review the PLOTDOSE SASLOG file.

```
R;
type plotdose saslog a  (col 2

          SAS(R) LOG  CMS SAS 5.08    ,  VM/CMS CMS USER USER11
NOTE: COPYRIGHT (C) 1984 SAS INSTITUTE INC., CARY, N.C.  27511, U.S.A.
NOTE: CMS SAS RELEASE 5.08 AT SAS INSTITUTE DATA CENTER (xxxxxxxx).

1          PROC PLOT DATA=DRUG432.MONITOR UNIFORM;
2            BY DOSE;
3            PLOT BACCNT*WEIGHT / VAXIS=0 TO 80 BY 2 HAXIS=100 TO 200 BY 10;
4            PLOT BACCNT*CHCKDATE / VAXIS=0 TO 80 BY 2;
5          RUN;

NOTE: SAS INSTITUTE, SAS CIRCLE, BOX 8000, CARY, N.C. 27511-8000
```

Screen 2.10 A SASLOG File Is TYPEd

BATCH EXECUTION MODE

Batch execution mode is typically used for SAS programs that take a long time to execute, particularly if they are programs that have to be executed on a regular basis. SAS programs run in a CMS batch machine are the same as SAS programs run in other modes; no special SAS statements or rules are used. Also, most CMS and CP commands can be used in a program submitted to a batch machine. Since batch programs are the same as other SAS programs, the discussion and examples in this companion focus on interactive and noninteractive modes of execution.

Refer to the *IBM Virtual Machine/System Product: CMS User's Guide* for details on submitting programs to CMS batch machines. In addition, use of CMS batch machines varies at different computer installations, so consult your installation's systems staff for information on using CMS batch processing at your site.

THE %INCLUDE STATEMENT

The SAS statement %INCLUDE allows you to use SAS statements stored in files at any place in a SAS program, whether using interactive or noninteractive execution. You can also "reuse" spooled lines of SAS statements from earlier in a SAS session with the %INCLUDE statement. (See the *SAS User's Guide: Basics, Version 5 Edition* for a complete discussion of %INCLUDE.)

The form of the %INCLUDE statement is

%INC *source* ... */options*;

where *source* is where the program looks for more SAS statements. Valid values for *source* are

- a CMS filename, if the filetype of the file is SAS.
- the filename of a MACLIB and a MACLIB member name in the form *filename(member)*.
- the fileref (DDname) of a file, if its filetype is something other than SAS.
- the fileref and member name of a member of an OS partitioned data set (assuming you can access the OS disk) in the form *fileref(member)*.
- the number (numbers) of a spooled line (lines) in the form *n:m*, where *n* is the first or only line and *m* is the last line.
- an asterisk (*) to indicate that execution should pause so that you can enter lines from the terminal.

These are examples using %INCLUDE:

`%INC PLOTDOSE;`	*(a CMS filename)*
`%INC STUDY5(MALES,FEMALES);`	*(the filename and members of a MACLIB)*
`%INC 12;`	*(the number of a spooled line)*
`%INC 12:25;`	*(a range of spooled lines)*
`%INC *;`	*(execution pauses for input from the terminal)*

When you reference a file in a %INCLUDE statement, the complete DATA and PROC steps in the source are scanned and executed. If the last DATA or PROC step in the source does not end with a RUN statement, that step is not executed until a RUN statement is entered or another DATA or PROC step is begun.

After %INCLUDEd statements have been processed

- in a display manager session, continue entering steps in the program editor, or browse output.
- in a line-mode session, SAS prompts you with a new line number so you can continue the session.
- in a noninteractive program, more statements can follow the %INCLUDE statement in the file.

Usage Notes

- You do not need to issue a FILEDEF for a file referenced in a %INCLUDE statement, if the filetype is SAS or MACLIB. The SAS System issues the FILEDEF automatically, regardless of the filemode.
- You must issue a FILEDEF for files that do not have filetype SAS or MACLIB if you want to specify them in a %INCLUDE statement.
- When you use the asterisk with %INCLUDE, you must also enter a %RUN statement to indicate when the terminal input is finished. The asterisk specification is most useful for noninteractive programs or nested %INCLUDEs.
- You cannot specify line numbers in the %INCLUDE statement unless the SAS system option SPOOL is in effect.
- In interactive SAS sessions, the %LIST statement is a convenient way to check spooled line numbers so you can specify them in a %INCLUDE statement.
- You can nest %INCLUDE statements.
- You can use %INCLUDE to process source files with line lengths greater than 80.

Screen 2.11 shows how you can use %INCLUDE in an interactive line-mode session. The name of the file referenced in the %INCLUDE statement is DOSECORR SAS A. Because the filetype is SAS, the filename is specified in the %INCLUDE statement (rather than a fileref) and no FILEDEF is needed. Notice how SAS flags the statements entered with %INCLUDE. Instead of the *n?* prompt, the line numbers are followed by a plus sign (+). The source of each %INCLUDEd line is shown below the line.

```
R;
sas (nodms
NOTE: COPYRIGHT (C) 1984 SAS INSTITUTE INC., CARY, N.C.  27511, U.S.A.
NOTE: CMS SAS RELEASE 5.08 AT SAS INSTITUTE DATA CENTER (xxxxxxxx).

  1?
%include dosecorr;
  1 %include dosecorr;
  2+proc corr data=drug432.monitor;
    1-//DOSECORR
  3+   var baccnt weight;
    1-//DOSECORR
  4+   by dose;
    1-//DOSECORR
  5+run;
    1-//DOSECORR
                               DOSE=200

VARIABLE      N      MEAN      STD DEV       SUM       MINIMUM     MAXIMUM

BACCNT       40  29.475000  23.2191207  1179.00000    0.000000   70.000000
WEIGHT       40  151.800000 23.9392393  6072.00000  108.000000  195.000000


    PEARSON CORRELATION COEFFICIENTS / PROB > |R| UNDER H0:RHO=0 / N = 40

                            BACCNT     WEIGHT


                 BACCNT    1.00000   -0.13678
                           0.0000     0.4000

                 WEIGHT   -0.13678    1.00000
                           0.4000     0.0000
```

Screen 2.11   Using %INCLUDE in a Line-Mode Session

INTERRUPTING SAS SESSIONS

You can interrupt your virtual machine during a line-mode session or a non-interactive SAS program when the terminal indicates that the virtual machine is in RUNNING status.* If you use a line-mode terminal, press the attention or break key to interrupt processing. If you use a full-screen terminal, use the ENTER key to interrupt processing.

After you interrupt processing during a SAS session, your terminal accepts a single line of input. You can:

- halt execution of the entire SAS session with the HX command. The SAS session terminates, and control returns to CMS. All FILEDEFs and most temporary WORK files are destroyed.**
- halt the display of output at the terminal for the current SAS step with the HT (halt typing) command. Terminal output for the current SAS step is canceled, but the SAS session continues, and FILEDEFs and WORK files remain intact. The output display resumes with the next DATA or PROC step or when an RT command is entered.

Note: the status of your SAS session after an interruption may depend on special features of your terminal or CMS installation. We assume you are using the default terminal mode setting:

```
CP TERMINAL MODE VM
```

---

* The method to use for interrupting a display manager session depends on your terminal and computer installation. Check with the local SAS software consultant for instructions.

** If any temporary files were written to disk, they are not destroyed.

for 327x terminals. (Use the CP command QUERY TERMINAL to confirm your terminal mode setting.) If you have problems interrupting processing, ask your CMS systems staff for help.

Interruption Due to System Failure

If your virtual machine is interrupted due to system problems and you are disconnected from your SAS session and return to CMS, resume your SAS session by entering a null line. If the system interruption causes you to return to CP, you can resume the SAS session by typing BEGIN.

CMS AND CP COMMANDS IN SAS PROGRAMS

Entering Commands during a SAS Session

There will probably be times when you want to issue CP and CMS commands from within a SAS session or program. For example, suppose you are in a line-mode SAS session and you want to access a file on another user's minidisk. In such a case you would want to issue the necessary LINK and ACCESS commands without leaving your SAS session.

You do not have to leave the SAS environment to enter a CMS or CP command. Three methods allow you to enter CMS and CP commands in the middle of a SAS session.

1. Invoke a single CMS or CP command by preceding the command with "CMS" and following it with a semicolon. (This is called a *CMS statement.*) The specified command is executed when SAS encounters the CMS statement as it scans a DATA or PROC step before execution.
2. Invoke *CMS subset mode* by using another form of the CMS statement. CMS subset mode provides an environment similar to the subset mode available under the CMS editor. To enter CMS subset mode, enter only:

   `CMS;`

   Once in the CMS subset you can invoke a series of CMS and CP commands before returning to SAS.
   When SAS scans the statements in the DATA or PROC step and encounters this kind of CMS statement, it enters CMS subset mode before any other SAS statements in that step are scanned.
3. Use the *CMS function*, which is a SAS function that invokes a single CMS or CP command as the SAS statements are executed. Because the CMS function is part of an executable SAS statement, it provides the facility to conditionally execute certain CMS and CP commands within a SAS session (unlike the CMS statement). Only CMS subset commands can be used with the CMS function.

Responses from CMS or CP to commands invoked within a SAS session are routed to the terminal, not to the SAS log or procedure output file. Responses are displayed immediately after the CMS statement in a line-mode SAS session. In a display manager session, the program editor/log screen is temporarily cleared, and the response displays on an otherwise blank screen; you must then press CLEAR or ALT/PA2 to return to display manager. For a noninteractive SAS program, responses are displayed at the terminal.

CMS Statement

A CMS statement invokes a CMS or CP command during a SAS session. The form of the statement is

CMS *CMScommand*;
CMS *CP CPcommand*;

The statement starts with the keyword CMS and ends with a semicolon. (CP commands can be preceded by "CP", but this is not required.)

CMS and CP commands in a CMS statement are executed when SAS scans the CMS statement.

A CMS statement can appear within a SAS DATA or PROC step or between steps. CMS statements within a step are scanned with that step. CMS statements between steps (that is, after a RUN statement but before the next DATA or PROC statement) are scanned before the next step.

There are no limitations to the CMS and CP commands allowed in the CMS statement, as long as you do not destroy your working environment. For example, you cannot issue a FORMAT command for the minidisk containing your current SAS WORK data library or an IPL command. Do not enter a FILEDEF * CLEAR command because it will clear FILEDEFs issued by the SAS System. You can use the CMS EXEC command to invoke an EXEC, as long as the EXEC does not include commands that would destroy your working environment.

Note: if the TLOG option has been specified, commands in subset mode are not written to the TLOG disk file.

Example

Screen 2.12 shows a SAS session in which CMS statements are used. A number of the CMS statements precede the first DATA step, so they are scanned and executed before SAS begins the DATA step. The commands are invoked to:

- LINK and establish ACCESS to another user's minidisk
- COPY a CMS file from the other user's disk to the A-disk
- RELEASE and DETACH the other user's disk.

In addition, there is a CMS FILEDEF command issued within the DATA step. The FILEDEF assigns a fileref (DDname) to a CMS file of input data. Because the FILEDEF executes as soon as it is scanned, the fileref is defined before SAS scans the INFILE statement that uses the fileref, as required by SAS syntax rules.

CMS Subset

To enter the CMS subset mode during a SAS session, issue a CMS statement that does not specify a CMS or CP command:

    CMS;

Once you are in the CMS subset mode, you can enter CMS and CP commands as if you were in the subset mode of the CMS editor. If you enter the CMS subset mode in the middle of a DATA or PROC step, the CMS and CP commands are invoked before SAS statements following the CMS statement are scanned.

```
  R;
  sas (nodms nosource
  NOTE: COPYRIGHT (C) 1984 SAS INSTITUTE INC., CARY, N.C.  27511, U.S.A.
  NOTE: CMS SAS RELEASE 5.08 AT SAS INSTITUTE DATA CENTER (xxxxxxxx).
  NOTE: CPUID   VERSION = FF   SERIAL = xxxxxx  MODEL = 4381 .

     1?
  cms cp link user11 191 192 rr;
  ENTER READ PASSWORD:

  DASD 192 LINKED R/O; R/W BY USER11
     2?
  cms access 192 b;
  DMSACC723I B (192) R/O
     3?
  cms copyfile drug doses b = = a (replace;
     4?
  cms release 192 (det;
  DASD 192 DETACHED
     5?
  data drug432.monitor;
     6?
    cms filedef dosedata disk drug doses a;
     7?
    infile dosedata;
     8?
```

Screen 2.12 Using CMS Statements

To return to SAS, enter:

RETURN

In the CMS subset mode, you are not prompted with a line number as you would expect during a SAS session. (The CMS subset prompt differs from installation to installation.) When you return to your SAS session from CMS subset mode, the numbering of SAS statements resumes where it left off.

If the TLOG system option is in effect, CMS and CP commands entered while in the CMS subset are not written to the TLOG disk file.

CMS Commands in Subset Mode

The CMS commands that can be used in subset mode are limited to the commands that do not use the *user area*. If you enter a command that is not allowed in subset mode, a message indicating that it is an invalid subset command is issued. See the *CMS User's Guide* for a list of commands that use the user area and, therefore, cannot be issued from subset mode.

CP Commands in Subset Mode

You can issue any CP command that does not destroy your working environment in CMS subset mode. For example, DEFINE STORAGE, FORMAT, and IPL cannot be used, but LINK, SPOOL, and TAG can be used.

Example

In **Screen 2.13** a series of CMS and CP commands is invoked from the CMS subset mode in the middle of a SAS session. This is an attempt to duplicate the series of commands entered with the CMS statement in **Screen 2.12**, but there are some differences. For example, the CMS COPYFILE command is not allowed in the CMS subset mode, so instead of copying the file to a minidisk, the file is read directly from the other user's disk.

```
R;
sas (nodms nosource
NOTE: COPYRIGHT (C) 1984 SAS INSTITUTE INC., CARY, N.C.  27511, U.S.A.
NOTE: CMS SAS RELEASE 5.08 AT SAS INSTITUTE DATA CENTER (xxxxxxxx).
NOTE: CPUID   VERSION = FF  SERIAL = xxxxxx  MODEL = 4381 .

   1?
cms;
CMS SUBSET

cp link user11 191 192 rr
ENTER READ PASSWORD:

DASD 192 LINKED R/O; R/W BY USER11
R;
access 192 b
DMSACC723I B (192) R/O
R;
copyfile drug doses b = = a
INVALID SUBSET COMMAND

return
   2?
data drug432.monitor;
   3?
    cms filedef dosedata disk drug doses b;
   4?
    infile dosedata;
   5?
```

Screen 2.13   Using CMS Subset Mode

CMS Function

The CMS function invokes one CMS or CP command and returns the return code set by execution of the command. The function is used as part of a SAS statement in the DATA step. For example, you might use the CMS function in an assignment statement:

   rc = CMS('*command*');

where

- *command* is a character string corresponding to a CMS or CP command
- *rc* is a variable that contains the return code set by execution of the command.

As part of an executable SAS statement, the CMS function allows you to conditionally execute CMS and CP commands within SAS. Commands invoked with the CMS function are executed when the DATA step executes, not when the statement containing the function is scanned.

The limitations on CMS and CP commands in subset mode also apply to the CMS function; that is, commands that use the user area are not allowed. Any CP commands that do not destroy your working environment can be issued.

Example

The sample SAS program below uses the CMS function. The program references five CMS files; each contains data for one weekday.

DAY1 DATA A
DAY2 DATA A
DAY3 DATA A
DAY4 DATA A
DAY5 DATA A

The first DATA step uses the TODAY and WEEKDAY SAS functions to construct a CMS FILEDEF for the CMS file containing data from the last weekday. For example, on Monday, a FILEDEF for Friday's data (CMS file DAY5 DATA A) is constructed. On Tuesday, a FILEDEF for Monday's data (CMS file DAY1 DATA A) is constructed. The FILEDEF is invoked with the CMS function. At execution time, the variable values inserted in the FILEDEF are resolved, and the FILEDEF is processed. When the CMS FILEDEF is successful, the return code value is zero.

Once the CMS FILEDEF has established a fileref (DDname) for the appropriate file, a SAS INFILE statement in the second DATA step can refer to that fileref.

```
DATA DAY;
   WD=WEEKDAY(TODAY())-2;
   IF WD=0 THEN WD=5;
   NUMBER=PUT(WD,1.);
   RETURN=CMS('FILEDEF DAILY DISK DAY'//NUMBER//' DATA A');
   PUT _ALL_;
RUN;
DATA DAILY;
   INFILE DAILY;
   INPUT BRANCH $ 1-20 DEPT 22-24 @26 REVENUE 10.;
RUN;
```

The sample program illustrates the differences between a command invoked with the CMS function and a command invoked with the CMS statement or in subset mode. Commands inserted with the CMS function are not invoked until execution time, after all statements in a step have been scanned, whereas commands inserted with a CMS statement or in subset mode are executed when SAS encounters them scanning the step. Since SAS resolves filerefs when statements are scanned (before execution), a fileref cannot be defined with the CMS function in the same DATA step in which it is used. A CMS function issuing a FILEDEF should precede the DATA step referencing the fileref.

Output and WORK Files

INTRODUCTION

The SAS System uses a number of files each time you run a SAS program, in addition to your data files or files of SAS programming statements. The required files include those containing the software, files for output, utility data sets, and so on. They are defined by FILEDEF commands that are issued automatically when you invoke the SAS System.* You can use the CMS command QUERY FILEDEF once you have started a SAS session to see which files have been defined automatically:

```
CMS QUERY FILEDEF;
```

---

* Because the SAS System issues FILEDEFs for a number of important files, you will destroy your working environment if you issue a FILEDEF * CLEAR command in a SAS session. You should clear FILEDEFs explicitly rather than by using the * specification.

QUERY FILEDEF lists the DDnames, devices, filenames, and filetypes for all files for which FILEDEFs have been issued. If you issue the QUERY FILEDEF command after invoking SAS, the listing includes any files you defined explicitly and the files defined automatically by the SAS System.

The files required for a SAS session can vary depending on the SAS software products licensed by your computer installation.* For example, suppose your installation licenses base SAS software and SAS/FSP and SAS/AF software. When you invoke the SAS System, FILEDEFs are issued automatically for these files:

DDname	Filename	Filetype	Contents
SASUTL			
$SYSLIB	SASBASE	LOADLIB	software
$SYSLIB	SASSERVR	LOADLIB	software
$SYSLIB	SASFSP	LOADLIB	software
$SYSLIB	SASAF	LOADLIB	software
$SYSLIB	SUGI	LOADLIB	software
SASLOG	SASLOG	SASLOG	SAS log, display manager
SASPROC	SASPROC	LISTING	procedure output, display manager
SASSRCE	SASSRCE	SAS	program editor screen contents, display manager
SASAUTOS	SASAUTOS	MACLIB	macro autocall library
SYSIN			
FT11F001	SAS	SASLOG	SAS log, line-mode and noninteractive
FT12F001	SAS	LISTING	procedure output, line-mode and noninteractive
FT13F001	SAS	SASPUNCH	PUNCH file
LIBRARY	xxxxxxxx	TEXT	for user-written formats
WORK	#DIRE	WORK	SAS WORK library
FT15F001	$SASPC	PARMCARD	PARMCARD file
SASHELP	SASHELP	MACLIB	SAS help files
SASMSGS	SASBMSG	MACLIB	SAS message files

Automatically defined files are used by the SAS System for a variety of purposes. Generally, you do not need to do anything with these files directly; they are "transparent" to the user. However, under some circumstances you may want to control some of these files yourself; for example, you may want to alter the default destination for the SAS log file. This chapter discusses the default files you need to know about for maximum flexibility in SAS programming. The files covered in this chapter are

- the SAS log file
- the SAS procedure output file
- the SAS PUNCH file

* In addition, your installation may have altered the definitions of some files.

- the PARMCARDS file
- the SAS WORK files.

THE SAS LOG FILE

The SAS log is one of two files of output produced by SAS programs. Every SAS program produces a log file; it contains processing notes, any error messages generated by the SAS System, and the SAS statements for each step.

By default, the SAS log goes to these destinations:

- For SAS programs executed from display manager, the SAS log displays in the log screen.
- In a line-mode SAS program, the SAS log displays at your terminal.
- In a noninteractive program, the SAS log is written to a disk file with filetype SASLOG and filemode A.

Display Manager

The SAS log in a display manager session is defined as the file SASLOG SASLOG, with DDname SASLOG. By default, the log is displayed on the log screen. However, you can also send the log to a disk file or a printer by using the display manager command PRINT. The form of the PRINT command to use for the SAS log is

PRINT [LOG] [*fileref*]

    LOG   is specified if you issue the PRINT command from the program editor screen or the output screen instead of the log screen. If you issue the PRINT command from the log screen, this specification is not necessary.

    fileref   is a DDname that has been defined previously with a CMS FILEDEF command. The fileref (DDname) references a disk file or the printer, depending on the definition of the file in the FILEDEF. If you specify a fileref that has not been defined previously with a FILEDEF command, an error message is issued.

        This specification is not required. If it is omitted, the log goes to a disk file called SASLOG SASLOG by default.*

Sending the Log to Disk

For example, suppose you have been working in a display manager session and you decide you want to save the SAS log in a disk file. If you issue this PRINT command from the log screen:

    `PRINT`

or this PRINT command from the program editor or output screen:

    `PRINT LOG`

the log goes to a disk file called SASLOG SASLOG A. To send the log to some other disk file, you must issue a FILEDEF before you issue the PRINT command. Then use the DDname specified in the FILEDEF as the fileref in the PRINT com-

---

* Your installation may have altered this default.

mand. For example, if you issue this FILEDEF:

```
CMS FILEDEF MYLOG DISK DRUG ANALYSIS (DISP MOD;
```

the log goes to disk when this PRINT command is issued from the log screen:

```
PRINT MYLOG
```

Notice that the DISP MOD parameter is specified in the FILEDEF. This allows you to send the log to the disk file repeatedly, without writing over existing records in the file. Without DISP MOD, the log from each SAS step is written over existing records, so only the log from the last SAS step is in the file at the end of the SAS session. Also note that if the FILEDEF specifies a file that does not already exist, you must include full DCB information in the FILEDEF.

Sending the Log to a Printer

To send the log to a printer, you must issue a FILEDEF before you issue the PRINT command. Then use the DDname specified in the FILEDEF as the fileref in the PRINT command. For example, if you issue this FILEDEF:

```
CMS FILEDEF LOGPRNT PRINTER;
```

the log goes to the spooled printer when this PRINT command is issued from the log screen:

```
PRINT LOGPRNT
```

Line-Mode and Noninteractive Sessions

The SAS log in a line-mode session or a noninteractive program is defined as a file with filetype SASLOG and DDname FT11F001. By default, the log from a line-mode session is displayed at the terminal; the log for a noninteractive program goes to a disk file. However, there are three SAS system options available to direct the SAS log to the destination of your choice.

LTYPE   routes the log to your terminal. (This is the default for a line-mode session.)

LDISK   routes the log to a disk file. The filetype is SASLOG and the filemode is A, but you can specify a filename with the NAME option. If the NAME option is not specified, the first filename in the SAS command is used in noninteractive programs, and the name SAS is used in line-mode sessions. (LDISK is the default setting for noninteractive programs.)

LPRINT   routes the log to the virtual printer.

For example, suppose you want to execute a line-mode SAS session and you want the log to go to a disk file. If you invoke SAS with this SAS command:

```
SAS (NODMS LDISK
```

a line-mode session begins, and the log is written to a disk file called SAS SASLOG A. To specify a filename other than SAS for the log file, add the NAME option to the SAS command. For example,

```
SAS (NODMS LDISK NAME MONDAY
```

causes the log to be written to a file called MONDAY SASLOG A.

You cannot specify LTYPE, LDISK, and LPRINT in an OPTIONS statement; you must specify them on the SAS command. These options do not apply to display manager sessions. In fact, if you specify any of them when invoking an interactive SAS session, you are forced into line-mode execution.

Multiple Destinations

You can specify multiple destinations for the SAS log by specifying more than one of the options LTYPE, LDISK, and LPRINT on the SAS command. For example, if you issue this SAS command:

```
SAS (NODMS LTYPE LDISK NAME MONDAY
```

you begin a line-mode session in which the log is displayed at the terminal as well as being sent to the disk file MONDAY SASLOG A.

When you route the log to the terminal and to the virtual printer or a CMS disk file, the output typed at the terminal has the same line length as if destined for the printer or a disk file; that is, the line size is determined by the SAS option LINESIZE, not TLINESIZE.

Messages at the Terminal

When the SAS log goes to a virtual printer or a CMS disk file but not to the terminal, it may be helpful to display an additional copy of the SAS error messages and processing notes at the terminal. The SAS system option TMSG allows you to determine which of three kinds of messages is displayed at the terminal when the SAS log is directed to a disk file or a printer:

TMSG ERRORS   displays SAS error messages at the terminal. This is the default setting.

TMSG NOTES   displays SAS error messages and processing notes at the terminal.

TMSG OFF   suppresses the display of any log information at the terminal.

Specify TMSG on the SAS command or in an OPTIONS statement. When TMSG is in effect, the complete text of an error message or note may not appear at the terminal. Consult the SAS log for the complete message.

Rerouting the Log during a Session

You cannot use the LDISK, LTYPE, and LPRINT options to reroute the log in the middle of a session because they can be specified only on the SAS command. However, you can send the SAS log to an alternate destination in the middle of a SAS session, if necessary, by using the CP SPOOL command.

SPOOL command   When the log is originally directed to the terminal, a SPOOL command can route a copy of it to the virtual card reader or to the virtual printer. The log continues to be displayed at the terminal. If the log is routed to the virtual printer, a TAG command is needed in addition to the SPOOL command to print the file.

When the log is originally directed to the virtual printer, you can use a CP SPOOL command to close the current printer file and a second CP SPOOL command to direct the remainder of the output to your virtual reader.

For example, if you are executing a line-mode session, the log is routed to the terminal by default. To capture the log at the reader after the session begins, first issue a SPOOL command:

```
CMS CP SPOOL CONSOLE TO * START;
```

Beginning immediately, the SAS log will be written to the virtual reader as well as to the terminal until you issue a second SPOOL command to close the spool file:

```
CMS CP SPOOL CONSOLE CLOSE STOP;
```

You do not need to issue the SPOOL CONSOLE CLOSE command from within the SAS session; you can also issue it after ending the SAS session.

Printing the Log

Carriage-control characters control line skipping and page ejects in output that is printed. These characters are automatically written in the first column of each line of the SAS log when:

- you use the display manager PRINT command
- the LPRINT option is in effect
- the LDISK option is in effect.

If you use the CMS PRINT command to print a SASLOG file, the carriage-control characters format the printed copy. Use the CC option in the PRINT command to indicate that the first column should be read as carriage-control. For example,

```
PRINT MONDAY SASLOG (CC
```

If you use the CMS command TYPE to display a SASLOG file at your terminal, the carriage-control characters are displayed and are not used for formatting. To prevent the carriage-control characters from being displayed when a SASLOG file is TYPEd, use the COL option in the TYPE command to specify that typing should begin in column two of the file. For example,

```
TYPE MONDAY SASLOG (COL 2
```

THE SAS PROCEDURE OUTPUT FILE

SAS procedure output is the other of the two files of output produced by SAS programs. This file contains any output generated by SAS procedures.* Although all SAS programs produce a SAS log file, some SAS programs may not produce a procedure output file.

By default, the destination of the procedure output file is

- the output screen in a display manager session.
- the terminal in a line-mode session.
- a disk file in a noninteractive program. By default, the filename of the disk file is the first filename specified on the SAS command. Or you can use the NAME option on the SAS command to assign a specific filename. The file has filetype LISTING, which is a special CMS filetype reserved for program output. The filemode is the same as the filemode of the SAS program unless the SAS program is on a disk accessed as read-only. If it is, the filemode is A by default.

Display Manager

The procedure output in a display manager session is defined as the file SASPROC LISTING, with DDname SASPROC. By default, the procedure output in a display manager session is routed to the output screen. However, you can also send the output to a disk file or printer by using the display manager command PRINT. The form of the PRINT command to use for the procedure output is

PRINT [OUTPUT] [*fileref*]

OUTPUT   is specified if you issue the PRINT command from the program editor screen or the log screen instead of the output screen. If you issue the PRINT command from the output screen, this specification is not necessary.

fileref   is a DDname that has been defined previously with a CMS FILEDEF command. The fileref (DDname) references a disk file or a printer, depending on the definition of the file in the FILEDEF. If you specify a fileref that has not been defined previously with a FILEDEF command, an error message is issued.

This specification is not required. If it is omitted, the output goes to a disk file called SASPROC LISTING by default.**

Sending Output to Disk

For example, suppose you have been working in a display manager session and you decide you want to save the procedure output in a disk file. If you issue this PRINT command from the output screen:

    PRINT

or this PRINT command from the program editor or log screen:

    PRINT OUTPUT

the output goes to a disk file called SASPROC LISTING A. To send the output to some other disk file, you must issue a FILEDEF before you issue the PRINT

---

* The procedure output file also contains records written by a SAS PUT statement if a FILE PRINT statement is in effect. See Chapter 5 for information on FILE PRINT.

** Your installation may have altered this default.

command. Then use the DDname specified in the FILEDEF as the fileref in the PRINT command. For example, if you issue this FILEDEF:

```
CMS FILEDEF MYOUT DISK DRUG ANALYSIS (DISP MOD;
```

the output goes to disk when you issue this PRINT command from the output screen:

```
PRINT MYOUT
```

Notice that the DISP MOD parameter is specified in the FILEDEF. This allows you to send output to the disk file repeatedly, without writing over existing records in the file. Without DISP MOD, output from each SAS step is written over existing records, so only the output from the last SAS step is in the file at the end of the SAS session.

Sending Output to a Printer

To send the output to a printer, you must issue a FILEDEF before you issue the PRINT command. Then use the DDname specified in the FILEDEF as the fileref in the PRINT command. For example, if you issue this FILEDEF:

```
CMS FILEDEF MYOUT PRINTER;
```

the output goes to the spooled printer when you issue this PRINT command from the output screen:

```
PRINT MYOUT
```

Line-Mode and Noninteractive Sessions

In line-mode sessions and noninteractive SAS programs, procedure output is defined as a file with filetype LISTING and DDname FT12F001. By default, the output is displayed at the terminal for line-mode sessions and is sent to a disk file for noninteractive programs. However, there are three SAS system options available for directing procedure output to the destination of your choice.

PTYPE   routes procedure output to your terminal. (This is the default setting for line-mode programs.)

PDISK   routes the procedure output to a disk file with filetype LISTING. (PDISK is the default setting for noninteractive mode.) The filename for the output file is the name you specify with the NAME option. If you do not use the NAME option, the first filename in the SAS command is used (for noninteractive programs), or the name SAS is used (for line-mode programs). In a noninteractive program, the LISTING file has the same filemode as the SAS program unless that minidisk is accessed in read-only mode. In a line-mode program, a LISTING file is written to the A-disk.

PPRINT   routes the procedure output to the virtual printer.

If you want SAS procedure output to be routed to something other than its default destination, use one or more of these options on the SAS command. For example, to route procedure output to a disk file during a line-mode session, use this SAS command:

```
SAS (NODMS PDISK
```

You cannot specify PTYPE, PDISK, and PPRINT in an OPTIONS statement; you must specify them on the SAS command. These options do not apply to display manager sessions.

Multiple Destinations

You can specify multiple destinations for procedure output by specifying more than one of the options PTYPE, PDISK, and PPRINT on the SAS command. For example, if you issue this SAS command:

```
SAS (NODMS PTYPE PDISK NAME MONDAY
```

you begin a line-mode session in which procedure output is displayed at the terminal as well as being sent to the disk file MONDAY LISTING A.

When you route output to the terminal and to the virtual printer or a CMS disk file, the output typed at the terminal has the same line length as if destined for the printer or a disk file; that is, the line size is determined by the SAS option LINESIZE, not TLINESIZE.

Rerouting Procedure Output during a Session

You can use the PDISK, PTYPE, and PPRINT options for routing the SAS procedure output only on the SAS command. However, you can reroute the procedure output file to an alternate destination during a SAS line-mode session or a non-interactive program, if necessary. There are three ways to reroute output after invoking SAS:

1. Issue a CMS FILEDEF command for FT12F001 from within your SAS session.
2. Use PROC PRINTTO.
3. Use the CP SPOOL command.

If you reroute output in the middle of a session, remember that the characteristics of printed output are influenced by the original destination. Therefore, if the original destination is the terminal and you switch to a CMS disk file, the line length of the output is still determined by the SAS system option TLINESIZE. (However, the CMS disk file will have carriage-control characters for page ejects and line skipping on a printer.)

Below are descriptions of the three methods to reroute procedure output during a session.

Redefine FT12F001 One way to change the output destination is to issue a CMS FILEDEF for DDname FT12F001, the output file between SAS steps. For example,

```
CMS FILEDEF FT12F001 DISK PROCS LISTING A
     (LRECL 137 RECFM VBA BLKSIZE 141 DISP MOD;
```

When you switch output to a CMS disk file (from the printer or terminal), specify the DISP MOD option in the FILEDEF command. Without DISP MOD, output from each SAS step is written over existing records, so only the output from the last SAS step is in the file at the end of the SAS session. You should also specify logical record length (LRECL 137), record format (RECFM VBA), and block size (BLKSIZE 141).

When you switch output to the virtual printer (from the terminal or a disk file), the printer spool file is closed at the end of each SAS step. This creates several printer spool files that will be printed separately. To write all the output to a single printer spool file, issue a SPOOL command with the CONT specification after the CMS FILEDEF associating FT12F001 with the printer. For example,

```
CMS CP SPOOL PRINTER CONT;
```

Then at the end of the SAS session, close the printer spool file with another SPOOL command:

```
CP SPOOL PRINTER NOCONT CLOSE
```

PROC PRINTTO You can invoke the PRINTTO procedure to reroute output from SAS procedures in the middle of a line-mode or noninteractive program. (Consult the *SAS User's Guide: Basics, Version 5 Edition* for a complete description of PRINTTO.)

Before you invoke PROC PRINTTO, first issue a CMS FILEDEF command for an alternate procedure output file. Assign a file number in the CMS FILEDEF instead of a DDname. Avoid file numbers 11, 12, 13, 14, and 15; these are reserved by the SAS System.

If you use PRINTTO to reroute output to a disk file, specify DISP MOD in the FILEDEF so that the output from each SAS step is added to the end of the file. Otherwise, the LISTING from each step is written over the LISTING from the previous step, and at the end of the session or program, the file contains output only from the last SAS step. You should also specify DCB characteristics: LRECL 137, BLKSIZE 141, and RECFM VBA. For example,

```
CMS FILEDEF 20 DISK X LISTING A
   (DISP MOD LRECL 137 BLKSIZE 141 RECFM VBA;
```

Once you issue the FILEDEF, direct procedure output to the alternate file by invoking the PRINTTO procedure. The form of the PROC PRINTTO statement is

PROC PRINTTO UNIT=*file number***;**

The UNIT= option in the PROC statement specifies the file number assigned to the alternate output file in the CMS FILEDEF.

To resume writing the procedure output to the original destination, invoke the PRINTTO procedure without the UNIT= option. For example,

```
PROC PRINTTO;
```

The SAS system option LINESIZE determines the line length SAS uses for procedure output routed to the alternative output file with the PRINTTO procedure.

SPOOL command You can also use the CP command SPOOL to reroute output in the middle of a SAS session. When procedure output is originally directed to the terminal, the CP SPOOL CONSOLE command can route a copy of the output to the virtual card reader or the virtual printer. (If output is routed to the virtual printer, use a TAG command to direct the file in the virtual printer to a real printer.)

When procedure output is originally directed to the virtual printer, use a CP SPOOL command to close the current printer file and a second CP SPOOL command to direct the remainder of the output to your virtual reader.

You cannot use the SPOOL command to reroute output if the current destination is a disk file.

Printing Procedure Output

Carriage-control characters control line skipping and page ejects in output that is printed. These characters are automatically written in the first column of each line of the procedure output when:

- you use the display manager PRINT command
- the PPRINT option is in effect
- the PDISK option is in effect.

If you print a LISTING file with the CMS PRINT command, the carriage-control characters format the file (you do not have to specify CC in the PRINT command). If you display a LISTING file by issuing a CMS TYPE command, the carriage-control characters are ignored. (You do not need the COL option in the TYPE command, as you do for the SASLOG file.)

Conflicting Destinations

When you route both the SAS log and the procedure output to disk, the log file and procedure output file are written to separate CMS files. However, if you send both to the virtual printer or to the terminal, the log and procedure output are interleaved, as in a line-mode session.

THE SAS PUNCH FILE

When you invoke SAS, a FILEDEF is automatically issued for the PUNCH file. PUNCH is a disk file identified by the DDname FT13F001, and its purpose is to contain records that can later be punched with the CMS PUNCH command. You may never need this file, even though it is defined each time you use the SAS System.

The DCB characteristics of the PUNCH file are

- logical record length = 80
- record format = F.

If records longer than 80 characters are written to the PUNCH file, the records are wrapped around to the next line.

The PUNCH file contains lines specified by a PUT statement if the corresponding FILE statement specifies the keyword PUNCH. (Refer to the *SAS User's Guide: Basics, Version 5 Edition* for more information on the FILE and PUT statements.) The PUNCH file's file-id is

filename SASPUNCH A

where *filename* is specified by the NAME option. If you do not use the NAME option, the first filename on the SAS command is assigned (noninteractive programs), or the filename SAS is assigned (interactive sessions).

THE PARMCARDS FILE

When you invoke SAS, a FILEDEF is automatically issued for the PARMCARDS file. This is a disk file identified by the DDname FT15F001. Parameter records that follow a PARMCARDS statement in a SAS PROC step are written to the PARMCARDS file.

The PARMCARDS file is most often needed in user-written procedures (for example, PROC EXPLODE in the SUGI supplemental library). The parameters written to the PARMCARDS file are retrieved from the PARMCARDS file by the procedure and are used for analysis.

Like the PUNCH file, you may never use the PARMCARDS file, even though it is defined each time you use the SAS System.

THE WORK SAS DATA LIBRARY

When you invoke SAS, a FILEDEF is issued automatically for files with the DDname and filetype WORK. These WORK files are a set of utility SAS files that are collectively called the *WORK data library*. The WORK data library is temporary. It is erased and initialized at the beginning of a SAS session and then erased at the end of a SAS session.

The SAS System cannot operate without the WORK library. It uses WORK to store utility files created during a SAS program, to contain the compiled program along with TITLE and FOOTNOTE lines, to store macros that have been defined, to store SPOOLed lines (if the SPOOL option is in effect), and so on.

In addition to SAS files generated by the SAS System, any temporary SAS files you create during a SAS program are written to the WORK library. That is, if you do not specify a first-level name when referencing a SAS file in SAS statements, SAS automatically uses WORK as the first-level name. (This is true unless you have already specified a default first-level name with the SAS system option USER=.) For example, in the following DATA step, SAS automatically assigns WORK as the first-level name of the new data set:

```
DATA DOSE300;
   SET DRUG432.MONITOR;
   IF DOSE=300;
```

Even though a one-level name is specified in the DATA statement, the name SAS uses internally for the new data set is WORK.DOSE300 (CMS file DOSE300 WORK). See Chapter 4, "CMS SAS Files," and the *SAS User's Guide: Basics, Version 5 Edition* for more information on naming SAS files.

By default, WORK files are kept in memory. However, if a SAS program or session generates more WORK files than can be stored in the memory allocated for the WORK library, additional files are written to disk.

The amount of memory allocated for the WORK library is a function of the size of the virtual machine, by default. To change the default you use the VIOBUF system option, which explicitly sets the number of 8K buffers of memory allocated for the WORK library. The lower the value specified for VIOBUF, the more likely it is that some WORK files will be written on disk. To force all WORK files to be written on disk, specify VIOBUF 0.

If some or all WORK files must be written to disk, they are written, by default, on the write-accessed minidisk having the most available free space when SAS is invoked. (However, you can specify a particular minidisk with the SAS system option SIODISK.) If you issue a LISTFILE command for the minidisk during a SAS session, you will see files with filetype WORK and filenames like #PROG and #DIRSPOL. These are some of the utility and system files used internally by SAS. You may also see WORK files that you created in the list.

Note: the WORK data library should not be saved because WORK files can become very large. This is especially true when the SAS system option SPOOL is in effect. If there are SAS files that you want to keep, be sure to make them permanent files rather than saving the entire WORK library.

CMS
SAS® Files

INTRODUCTION

The SAS System divides files into two basic categories: *SAS files* and *external files*.

- *SAS files* can be created and processed only with SAS programs, not with other programming languages or software. SAS files are specially structured with characteristics that make them efficient and convenient for the SAS System to process. Many SAS procedures can analyze and manipulate data only in the form of a SAS file.
- *External files* can be created and processed by other languages or software, as well as by SAS programs. Files containing SAS programs, VSAM files, MACLIBs, and TXTLIBs are examples of external files.

This chapter discusses using SAS files in CMS SAS programs. See Chapter 5 for information on external files in CMS SAS programs.

Many topics mentioned in this chapter, such as SAS data set options and SAS utility procedures, are documented in the *SAS User's Guide: Basics, Version 5 Edition*. If you are not familiar with these SAS features, be sure to read about them in the *Basics* manual. Also, consult the **REFERENCES** section at the end of Chapter

1 for the appropriate documentation on the CMS and CP commands mentioned in this chapter.

WHAT IS A SAS FILE?

Under CMS, a SAS file is a specially structured CMS file. Although CMS manages the file for the SAS System by storing it, CMS cannot actually process the file because of the unique characteristics the SAS System builds into SAS files. For example, the CMS FILELIST command can list SAS file-ids, but a CMS editor cannot be used to modify or read a SAS file.

Any SAS file can be temporary (used in only one program or session) or permanent (stored on disk or tape to be used again). The name of a SAS file determines whether it is temporary or permanent, as discussed in **CMS SAS FILE NAMES**.

Types of SAS Files

There are a number of different kinds of SAS files. The most commonly used SAS file is the *SAS data set*, which contains *observations* for which *variable values* have been recorded. The sample SAS data set described in Chapter 1, DRUG432.MONITOR, is an example of this kind of SAS file.

Other kinds of SAS files are described below:*

- A *catalog* is a SAS file containing one or more *entries*. The entries can be user function key profiles for display manager and full-screen editing facilities, screens for SAS/AF and SAS/FSP software, FSCALC procedure spreadsheets, and SAS/GRAPH software templates. See the appendix on full-screen editing in the *SAS User's Guide: Basics, Version 5 Edition* and also the *SAS/FSP User's Guide, Version 5 Edition* and the *SAS/AF User's Guide, Version 5 Edition* for details on catalogs.
- *Graphics catalogs* contain graphs produced by SAS/GRAPH software. See the *SAS/GRAPH User's Guide, Version 5 Edition* for complete information.
- *Work space files* contain saved work space from SAS/IML software. See the *SAS/IML User's Guide, Version 5 Edition* for details.
- *Model files* contain models generated by SAS/ETS software. See the *SAS/ETS User's Guide, Version 5 Edition* for details.

SAS data sets and catalogs are used with base SAS software and other SAS software. Graphics catalogs and workspace and model files are used with products other than base SAS software. You might have applications for all types of SAS files, or you might need just one or two types. All kinds of SAS files can be managed by base SAS software's utility procedures: CONTENTS, COPY, and DATASETS.

Each kind of SAS file has a corresponding keyword to identify its type. These keywords are used by the CONTENTS, COPY, and DATASETS utility procedures. The keywords for the different types are

CAT	catalog
DATA	SAS data set
GCAT	graphics catalog

---

* In addition to the files listed here, there are several kinds of SAS files used only for maintenance and internally by the SAS System. In particular, there are a number of files with CMS filetype SASUTL. These files are necessary for SAS execution, but they are not meant to be accessed by users. Do not try to update or erase any file with CMS filetype SASUTL.

IMSWK   SAS/IML saved work space

MODEL   SAS/ETS model

When you create a catalog, graphics catalog, work space file, or model file, SAS attaches a one-character prefix to the second-level name (the CMS filename) and passes the prefixed name to CMS. The purpose of the prefix is to distinguish the different types of SAS files for CMS; for example, the prefix attached to a catalog's name is "5". In SAS statements and commands you do not use the prefix, only the filename. However, in CMS commands, you must specify the prefix, and CMS displays the prefix when it references the file.

For example, suppose you create a catalog called DRUG432.DATASCR (CMS file 5DATASCR DRUG432) that contains FSEDIT screens as entries. In a PROC FSEDIT statement you can specify the filename without the prefix. For example,

```
PROC FSEDIT DATA=DRUG432.DOSES SCREEN=DRUG432.DATASCR;
```

When the CMS FILELIST command lists this catalog in a file list, it displays the prefix. So the filename appears as "5DATASCR". To erase the file with the CMS command ERASE, you would specify the prefix:

```
ERASE 5DATASCR DRUG432 A
```

CMS SAS FILE NAMES

A SAS file is named when it is created. For example, a SAS data set is named in the DATA statement if it is being created by a DATA step.

CMS and the SAS System use different syntax rules to identify a file.

- CMS identifies a SAS file as it does all files, with a three-part name consisting of the filename, filetype, and filemode, for example, MONITOR DRUG432 A.
- The SAS System identifies a SAS file by a name consisting of two words separated by a period, for example, DRUG432.MONITOR. The first part of the name is the *libref*, also called the first-level name. The second part of the name is the filename or the second-level name.

The SAS libref corresponds to the CMS filetype. It is also the DDname assigned to a file in a FILEDEF command. The second-level SAS name is the same as the CMS filename. So the SAS file DRUG432.MONITOR is the CMS file MONITOR DRUG432. Assuming that the file is stored on the A-disk, the FILEDEF for the file would look like this:

```
FILEDEF DRUG432 DISK MONITOR DRUG432 A
```

Nothing in the SAS name corresponds to the CMS filemode.

In this book, the terms libref, DDname, filetype, and first-level name are interchangeable, and filename and second-level name are interchangeable.

The libref for any SAS file can be up to eight characters in length. Filenames for SAS data sets can be eight characters long, but filenames for other kinds of SAS files are limited to seven characters because the one-character prefix must be attached. Apart from this length restriction for filenames, the other rules for valid SAS names and CMS names apply to SAS files.

The Libref

The name you choose to be a libref determines whether a SAS file is temporary or permanent. By default, if the libref is WORK, the file is temporary. If you assign any other libref, the file is permanent.

The purpose of the libref is to point to a storage location: a minidisk, tape, or work space in memory. The SAS System knows which storage location a libref references because the libref is *defined*. For most disk files and for all WORK files, the SAS System defines the libref automatically. For tape SAS files (and occasionally for disk files), you define the libref with a FILEDEF command. The rules for defining librefs for permanent SAS files are discussed in later sections of this chapter on disk and tape SAS files.

SAS Data Library Concept

More than one SAS file can have the same libref (filetype). All SAS files with the same libref are *members* of the same *SAS data library* if they are on the same minidisk or tape.* For example, all WORK files from a particular program or session are members of the WORK SAS data library. There is no limit to the number of members in a SAS data library.

The SAS data library is a logical concept allowing you to group related SAS files in one place and to reference them with one libref. The SAS utility procedures CONTENTS, COPY, and DATASETS are designed to take advantage of the SAS data library concept. These three procedures can process multiple SAS files in one step, as long as they are all members of the same library.

Assigning Names to SAS Files

SAS files are named in several ways:

1. You can specify both names in a SAS statement referencing the file. For example,

   ```
   DATA MY.SASDATA;
   PROC FSEDIT DATA=MY.SASDATA SCREEN=MY.SCREENS;
   PROC SORT DATA=MY.SASDATA OUT=MY.SORTED;
   ```

   Because the libref for these files **is not** WORK, the files are permanent SAS files.
2. You can specify only one name in a SAS statement. If you specify one name, SAS assumes that it is the second-level name and uses WORK as the libref by default.** Therefore, the file is a temporary file. For example, when SAS processes this statement:

   ```
   PROC FSEDIT DATA=WEIGHTS SCREEN=WGHTSCR;
   ```

   SAS assumes that you are referencing the SAS files WORK.WEIGHTS and WORK.WGHTSCR and that they are temporary files.
3. For SAS data sets only, if you omit a name specification altogether, SAS assigns default names for both names. By default, the libref is WORK, and the second-level name is DATA*n*, where *n* is 1 for the first data set created in the SAS program, 2 for the second, and so on. For example, this DATA step creates the SAS data set WORK.DATA1:

   ```
   DATA;
       INPUT X Y;
       CARDS;
   data lines
   ```

---

* A SAS data library can exist on two or more minidisks if the second (third, and so on) minidisk is accessed as a read-only extension of the first minidisk.

** The default libref can be changed with the USER SAS system option or the WORK SAS system option.

Important notes:

- Do not use a libref that is used by the SAS System as a reserved DDname. The reserved DDnames are

FT11F001	LIBRARY	SYSIN
FT12F001	SASDUMP	$SYSLIB
FT13F001	SASLIB	SYSOUT
FT14F001	SORTWKxx	WORK
FT15F001	SORTLIB	

- Do not use SAS as a libref; it is reserved as the filetype for files of SAS programming statements used in noninteractive SAS programs and with %INCLUDE.
- Do not use a CMS reserved filetype as a libref. (The CMS reserved filetypes are listed in the *CMS User's Guide*.)
- Do not use the filetype of a non-SAS file (external file) as the libref/filetype of a SAS file.
- Librefs beginning with "TAPE" are reserved for SAS files written in tape format.
- When you create a SAS file that has the same file-id as an existing SAS file, SAS creates a new CMS file for the new SAS file and erases the old file with the same name by default. (For disk-format files, the files must be on the same minidisk.) The default can be overridden by the REPLACE | NOREPLACE SAS system option or, for SAS data sets only, the REPLACE= data set option.

Disk or Tape?

Permanent SAS files can be stored on disk or tape. Each storage method has its advantages and disadvantages. Here are some points to keep in mind when deciding whether to use disk or tape:

- Accessing tapes is usually slower and more cumbersome than accessing files on disk because the tapes must be mounted by the operator.
- For nonlabeled tapes you must position the tape to the correct file unless you are accessing the first file on the tape.
- If a SAS file on tape is modified or deleted, any file that follows cannot be accessed.
- Tapes are able to accommodate large files for which disk storage is impractical.
- CMS SAS files in tape format can be read by the SAS System under OS and VSE. (See Appendix 3 for information on transporting CMS SAS files to the SAS System under AOS/VS, PRIMOS, and VMS.)

SAS FILES ON CMS MINIDISKS

Each disk-format SAS file is stored as a separate CMS file, with the libref corresponding to both DDname and filetype. The second-level name corresponds to the filename. (Note: SAS files can also be stored in tape-format on disk. See **CMS SAS FILES IN TAPE FORMAT** later in this chapter.)

Writing SAS Files

To write a disk-format SAS file, you usually only need to specify the file's two-level name in the appropriate SAS statement. Under most circumstances, you do not have to issue a FILEDEF to define a libref because the SAS System automatically defines librefs for permanent SAS files on disk. For example, to create a sorted version of DRUG432.MONITOR using the OUT= option of PROC SORT, you could use this PROC step:

```
PROC SORT DATA=DRUG432.MONITOR OUT=DRUG432.DOSESORT;
   BY DOSE AGE;
RUN;
```

This is the process the SAS System follows for a SAS file that is being created (written) on disk:

- When SAS encounters a libref while scanning a SAS statement, the SAS System checks the list of current FILEDEFs to see if that libref has been defined already as a DDname. If it has already been defined, SAS writes the new SAS file to the minidisk indicated by the FILEDEF.
- If the libref is not defined by a current FILEDEF, SAS searches all accessed minidisks to see if there are any SAS files with filetypes that match the libref. If a matching filetype is found, SAS writes the file to the minidisk containing the SAS file with a matching filetype (unless the minidisk is accessed as read-only, in which case an error message is issued).
- If no matching filetype is identified, SAS writes the file to the A-disk, using the libref as the filetype.

There is only one case in which you must issue a FILEDEF defining a libref before you write a SAS file on disk: when SAS System defaults will cause the file to be written to a minidisk other than the one you want to use. Remember that the defaults are a minidisk referenced by a current FILEDEF for that libref, a minidisk containing a file of the same filetype, or the A-disk.

When you have to issue a FILEDEF for a SAS file, you can use this form of the command:

FILEDEF *DDname* DISK *dummy dummy filemode*

where *DDname* is the libref you want to use for the file and *filemode* references the correct minidisk for the file. Notice that *dummy* is specified in the filename and filetype positions on the command. This is because you can specify any valid character string for these parameters, and SAS will substitute the correct filename and filetype. Thus, you need to issue only one FILEDEF command per libref, regardless of the number of SAS files that have or will have that libref.

For example, suppose you want to write a SAS data set called DRUG432.DOSE250 to your B-disk (CMS file DOSE250 DRUG432 B) and that the SAS data set DRUG432.MONITOR is on your C-disk (CMS file MONITOR DRUG432 C). If you **do not** issue a FILEDEF, SAS will find the file with filetype DRUG432 on your C-disk and will write the new SAS data set to the C-disk. To write the new SAS data set to the B-disk, you should issue a FILEDEF explicitly. For example,

```
FILEDEF DRUG432 DISK DUMMY DUMMY B
```

Reading SAS Files

When you want to read an existing CMS SAS file, you usually only need to specify its name in the correct SAS statement; you do not have to issue a FILEDEF defining the libref in most cases. For example, to read an existing SAS data set in a DATA step, just reference the file in a SET, MERGE, or UPDATE statement, as shown in this DATA step:

```
DATA DRUG432.DOSE250;
   SET DRUG432.MONITOR;
   IF DOSE=250;
RUN;
```

When SAS encounters a libref for a file to be read, it follows these steps:

1. SAS searches for a current FILEDEF for the libref. If one is found, SAS searches the minidisk indicated by the FILEDEF for the SAS file.
2. If there is no current FILEDEF for the libref, SAS searches (in standard minidisk search order) all accessed minidisks for a SAS file with matching filename and filetype.

The only time you must issue a FILEDEF to read an existing SAS file on a CMS disk is when SAS System defaults will cause the file to be read from a minidisk other than the one you want to use. In other words, if there are multiple files with the same filename and filetype on different minidisks, SAS will read the file on the minidisk that comes first in the search order. To read a SAS file on a disk later in the search order, you need to issue a FILEDEF explicitly.

For example, suppose you have two files named DRUG432.SCREEN: one on your A-disk and one on your B-disk (CMS files SCREEN DRUG432 A and SCREEN DRUG432 B). You want to use the one on the B-disk. When SAS searches the accessed minidisks for a matching file, it will find the file on the A-disk first and stop searching. Therefore, you will have to issue a FILEDEF for the B-disk:

```
FILEDEF DRUG432 DISK DUMMY DUMMY B
```

As is the case when writing SAS files, you can use any words for the filename and filetype specification. The SAS System will subsitute the correct values. This means you need only one FILEDEF per libref, regardless of the number of files with the libref.

CMS SAS FILES IN TAPE FORMAT

Under CMS, SAS files can be stored in *tape* or *sequential format*. Tape-format files can be stored on real tape or on disk.

SAS files in tape format are not as flexible as SAS files in disk format.

- With tape-format SAS files, you cannot access more than one file at a time. This means you cannot merge or concatenate two or more tape-format SAS data sets.
- You cannot use the EDITOR procedure for SAS data sets stored in tape format because EDITOR uses direct-access methods as opposed to sequentially processing one observation after another. Likewise, you cannot use the SAS/FSP procedure FSEDIT to process a tape-format data set.
- SAS data sets in tape format cannot be accessed randomly with the POINT= and NOBS= variables on the SET statement.
- There are no facilities to rename SAS files in tape format.

- Whether you are using tape or disk, each SAS file in tape format is stored as a single, physical file, as long as each file has a unique libref. **If you write more than one SAS file in tape format using the same libref, they will be written as one physical, sequential file.**
- If you replace or delete an existing tape-format disk SAS file that is in a sequential file with other SAS files, any SAS file that follows in the sequential file can no longer be accessed. This restriction is extended for SAS files on real tape. **All** files on the tape following the affected SAS file become inaccessible.

The libref of a tape-format SAS file **must** begin with the characters TAPE. **Never use a DDname beginning with TAPE for non-SAS files** of any kind.

CMS SAS Files on Tape

The CMS SAS System uses the tape-handling facilities of CMS to process tape files.* **Before you use tape files, be sure to read about tape processing under CMS** in the *CMS User's Guide* and the *CMS Command and Macro Reference*.

Warning: **never write to a tape if you are unsure of its contents and their order.** Tape files can be destroyed quite easily by accidental overwriting. You should also be sure that you are familiar with the effects of CMS tape positioning commands and options such as the SAS data set option FILEDISP=.

When you write a SAS file on a tape that already contains files, be aware that overwriting an existing file causes any files that follow it to be inaccessible. If you want to preserve existing files on a tape, you must write new files **after** existing files.

To read or write a SAS file on tape, follow these steps:

1. First arrange to have the tape mounted and attached to your virtual machine. Some installations have special commands for tape mounts; others require that you send a message to the operator. Some installations do not allow CMS users to access tapes at all. Ask your SAS software consultant or other installation personnel about how to have tapes mounted at your installation.

   When the tape is attached to your virtual machine, you usually receive a message noting the virtual address of the tape.
2. If the tape is nonlabeled, position it with CMS TAPE commands. If the tape is a new, labeled tape, write the volume label with a CMS TAPE command.
3. Issue a CMS FILEDEF to associate the tape with a libref. For example,

   ```
   FILEDEF DDname TAPn labeloperands
   ```

   Notice that you do not need to specify filename, filetype, or filemode on the tape FILEDEF. Remember that the libref must begin with TAPE. There is no filename, filetype, or filemode specified for files on a real tape. If the tape is labeled, be sure the correct label-processing operands are specified on the FILEDEF. This ensures that the tape is positioned correctly.
4. Then reference the file in the appropriate SAS statement, where the libref corresponds to the DDname in the CMS FILEDEF pointing to the tape.

When you write more than one SAS file on a tape, remember that each SAS file is a single tape file as long as different librefs are used for each SAS file. A tape SAS data library containing more than one member is just one tape file.

---

* The CMS SAS System **does not** support multivolume tapes.

At the end of a DATA or PROC step writing a tape file, SAS closes the tape file, and CMS writes a tapemark. (Some versions of CMS may not write the tape-marks when a file is closed; check with your installation personnel.)

Notes on Nonlabeled Tapes

If the tape you are accessing is nonlabeled, it must be positioned to the correct file before you can read or write a SAS file. To position a tape, use CMS TAPE commands for rewinding (REW), forward spacing (FSF), and backward spacing (BSF), after the tape is mounted.

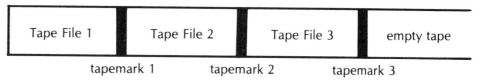

Figure 4.1   A Sample Nonlabeled Tape Layout

Refer to **Figure 4.1** as you follow the discussion below:

- TAPE REW rewinds the tape to the beginning. You should routinely rewind a tape before writing to it so you know exactly where the tape is positioned before trying to forward space and backward space.
- TAPE FSF moves the tape forward *n* tapemarks:

    TAPE FSF *n*

    The tape is positioned immediately after the last counted tapemark. For example, suppose you are using a tape with three tapemarks, the last of which is at the end of the last file on the tape (see figure). Use this TAPE command to position the tape after the last tapemark (assuming the tape is originally positioned at the beginning):

    TAPE FSF 3

- TAPE BSF moves the tape backward *n* tapemarks:

    TAPE BSF *n*

    The tape is positioned immediately in front of the last counted tapemark. In the example for forward spacing, the tape was left positioned after the last of three tapemarks on the tape. To backward space so that the tape is positioned **before** the second tapemark, issue this command:

    TAPE BSF 2

Notes on Labeled Tapes

The SAS System uses CMS facilities for labeled-tape processing. To read or write a labeled tape, be sure the FILEDEF for the file indicates the correct operands for label processing. For example, for a standard-labeled tape file, the FILEDEF should have this form:

FILEDEF *DDname* TAP*n* SL *p*

where *p* is the position of the file to be read or written (the default is 1). As long as you specify the correct FILEDEF information for label processing, you do not have to position the tape.

When you write to a labeled tape, CMS creates the file's label if it does not already exist.

Before writing to a new, blank tape, issue a TAPE WVOL1 command to write the volume label.

FILEDISP= Data Set Option

When writing a new SAS data set on tape, you must be aware of the effects of the SAS data set option FILEDISP=. The FILEDISP= data set option tells SAS whether the data set being written is a member of an existing SAS data library on the tape or is the first member of a new library.

If FILEDISP=OLD (the default) is in effect, SAS assumes that you are writing a member to an existing SAS data library and that the tape is already positioned at that library (that is, at that tape file). First, SAS searches the tape for a member of the same name. If a matching member is found, SAS writes the new data set over the existing data set. If SAS does not find a matching member but does find a tapemark, it assumes that it has come to the end of the library. SAS then writes the new SAS data set, writing over the tapemark. In other words, it adds the new data set to the end of the library. If SAS finds neither a matching member nor a tapemark, the tape runs off the end of the reel. Do not use FILDISP=OLD unless you are writing to an existing library.

If you specify FILEDISP=NEW, SAS assumes that you are creating a new library and that the tape is positioned correctly. SAS writes the SAS data set wherever the tape is positioned, without looking for an existing file or a tapemark. Therefore, unless you are using a blank tape or want to overwrite a file, you should position the tape **after** the last file and tapemark on the tape.

If a SAS data set is written with FILEDISP=NEW, the SAS System will not write over it as long as the FILEDEF for that file is in effect. This is true even if you write more data sets to that library with FILEDISP=NEW. However, if you clear the FILEDEF or re-issue it for another file, the SAS data set can be overwritten.

Examples

In the first SAS program below, a SAS data set is written on a nonlabeled tape that already contains one member of the same SAS data library. Assume that the tape has already been mounted, but not rewound and positioned. FILEDISP=OLD, the default, is in effect, so a TAPE FSF command is issued to position the tape after the leading tapemark and before the first member in the library. The DATA step writes the SAS data set on the tape **after** the existing SAS file.

```
CMS TAPE REW;
CMS TAPE FSF;
CMS FILEDEF TAPESDS TAP1;
DATA TAPESDS.D432BU;
   SET DRUG432.MONITOR;
RUN;
```

In the next example, a nonlabeled tape already contains two external files. FILEDISP=NEW is specified for the SAS data set so the tape must be forward-spaced, or SAS would write over the existing files.

```
TAPE REW;
CMS TAPE FSF 3;
CMS FILEDEF TAPEDATA TAP3;
DATA TAPEDATA.SCORES (FILEDISP=NEW);
   INPUT STUDENT $11. TEST1 3.0 TEST2 3.0 TEST3 3.0 TEST4 3.0;
   CARDS;
...data lines...
RUN;
```

In the third example, a SAS data library is created on a new tape that will have standard labels. The TAPE WVOL1 command writes the volume label at the beginning of the tape, and the FILEDEF command includes the SL and position label operands. FILEDISP=NEW is specified because a new library is created.

```
CMS TAPE REW;
CMS TAPE WVOL1 VM6111;
CMS FILEDEF TAPEBANK TAP1 SL 1;
DATA TAPEBANK.NCYIELD (FILEDISP=NEW);
   SET AGRI.NCYIELD;
RUN;
```

In the next example, a SAS data set is read from a standard-labeled tape. It is the second file on the tape.

```
CMS FILEDEF TAPEFILE TAP2 SL 2;
PROC PRINT DATA=TAPEFILE.MONITOR;
   VAR WEIGHT AGE INITBAC BACCNT CHCKDATE;
   ID SUBJECT;
   BY DOSE;
```

CMS SAS Files on Disk in Tape Format

SAS files can be stored on disk in tape format under CMS SAS. Keep the limitations of tape-format SAS files in mind when choosing between tape format and disk format. The sequential nature of the tape format does have limitations, but tape-format SAS files can be processed by some other operating systems' versions of SAS.

As with SAS files on tape, each disk SAS file in tape format is stored as a single file as long as each SAS file has a unique libref. If you write multiple disk SAS files in tape format using the same libref, they are all written to one sequential file, making access to a particular SAS file difficult.

To force tape format for a SAS file on disk, begin the libref with the characters TAPE. If no current FILEDEF exists for the libref, SAS issues one automatically:

```
FILEDEF libref DISK SASTAPE filetype A
```

The file is written to the A-disk with the default filename SASTAPE.

Be sure to issue a FILEDEF yourself if you want the file to be on a minidisk other than the A-disk. You must specify the correct filename and filetype for tape-format disk data sets, not dummy specifications.

The following SAS program writes two tape-format SAS data sets on disk.

```
CMS FILEDEF TAPEDAY1 DISK EARN TAPEDAY1 A;
CMS FILEDEF IN1 DISK EARN DAY1;
DATA TAPEDAY1.EARN;
   INFILE IN1;
   INPUT BRANCH $ 1-20 DEPT 22-24 @26 REVENUE 10.;
RUN;
CMS FILEDEF TAPEDAY2 DISK EARN TAPEDAY2 A;
CMS FILEDEF IN2 DISK EARN DAY2;
DATA TAPEDAY2.EARN;
   INFILE IN2;
   INPUT BRANCH $ 1-20 DEPT 22-24 @26 REVENUE 10.;
RUN;
```

The next example reads the tape-format SAS data sets created in the previous example.

```
PROC PRINT DATA=TAPEDAY1.EARN;
   ID BRANCH;
   VAR REVENUE DEPT;
RUN;
PROC PRINT DATA=TAPEDAY2.EARN;
   ID BRANCH;
   VAR REVENUE DEPT;
RUN;
```

CMS SAS FILE MANAGEMENT

A number of SAS utility procedures that facilitate file management are available. They are described briefly in this section. For complete discussions of these and other utility procedures, see the *SAS User's Guide: Basics, Version 5 Edition*.

Documenting the Contents of SAS Data Sets

The CONTENTS procedure can list all SAS files in a SAS data library. CONTENTS also retrieves the descriptor information at the beginning of a SAS data set.

To compare the file information available from the CMS command LISTFILE and that from PROC CONTENTS, see **Screens 4.1** and **4.2**. **Screen 4.1** shows file information displayed by the CMS LISTFILE command. **Screen 4.2** shows the directory information retrieved by PROC CONTENTS for the same group of files and the directory information for one of the SAS data sets in the library.

```
USER11    FILELIST A0 V 108 TRUNC=108 SIZE=5 LINE=1 COL=1 ALT=0
Cmd    Filename Filetype FM Format Lrecl    Records    Blocks   Date      Time
       6GRAPHS  MONTHLY  C1 F      1024         11         6 12/18/85 16:37:49
       MAR      MONTHLY  C1 F      1024          2         1 12/18/85 16:37:13
       5SCREEN  MONTHLY  C1 F      1024          2         1 12/18/85 16:37:04
       FEB      MONTHLY  C1 F      1024          2         1 12/18/85 16:37:05
       JAN      MONTHLY  C1 F      1024          2         1 12/18/85 16:37:09




    1= Help     2= Refresh  3= Quit    4= Sort(type)   5= Sort(date)  6= Sort(size)
    7= Backward 8= Forward  9= FL/n   10=             11= XEDIT       12= Cursor
```

Screen 4.1 Sample Output from the FILELIST Command

```
SAS

CONTENTS PROCEDURE
SAS DATA LIBRARY DIRECTORY


NAME         MEMTYPE      #OBS


FEB          DATA         7
GRAPHS       GCAT
JAN          DATA         6
MAR          DATA         4
SCREEN       CAT


CONTENTS OF SAS MEMBER MONTHLY.FEB


CREATED BY CMS USERID USER11   ON CPUID XX-XXXX-XXXXXX   AT 16:34 WEDNESDAY,
DECEMBER 18, 1985   BY SAS RELEASE 5.08

FILE= MONTHLY FEB   BLKSIZE=8176   LRECL=36   GENERATED BY DATA
NUMBER OF OBSERVATIONS: 7   NUMBER OF VARIABLES: 4
MEMTYPE:   DATA

----ALPHABETIC LIST OF VARIABLES AND ATTRIBUTES-----
       # VARIABLE TYPE   LENGTH POSITION FORMAT       INFORMAT    LABEL
       3 AGE      NUM       8      20
       1 EMPLOYEE CHAR      8       4
       2 SALARY   NUM       8      12
       4 STATUS   CHAR      8      28



--------------------------------- SOURCE RECORDS ---------------------------
| DATA MONTHLY.FEB;                                                          |
|     INPUT EMPLOYEE $ SALARY AGE STATUS $;                                  |
|     CARDS;                                                                 |
----------------------------------------------------------------------------
```

Screen 4.2 Sample Output from PROC CONTENTS

Copying SAS Files

The best way to copy SAS files is with the SAS COPY procedure. However, with some limitations it is also possible to use CMS commands. CMS commands cannot convert SAS files to and from tape format; they are not sensitive to DDnames beginning with TAPE.

- COPYFILE can copy SAS files from minidisk to minidisk.
- MOVEFILE can copy SAS files from minidisk to minidisk, from tape to tape, from minidisk to tape, or from tape to minidisk. If you move a disk-format SAS file to tape with MOVEFILE, the SAS file cannot be accessed until it is moved back to minidisk.
- DISK DUMP punches a SAS file to the virtual card punch. DISK LOAD restores a file punched with DISK DUMP to its original form.
- TAPE DUMP dumps disk files to tape. TAPE LOAD restores tape files written by TAPE DUMP to disk. If you dump any SAS file to tape with TAPE DUMP, the SAS file cannot be accessed until it is restored to minidisk with TAPE LOAD.

Deleting SAS Files

The SAS procedure DATASETS deletes disk-format SAS files. (In addition to deleting SAS files, DATASETS can rename disk-format SAS data sets.)

You can also use the CMS ERASE command to delete some or all members of a SAS data library created under Release 82.3 or Version 5. For example,

```
ERASE filename filetype filemode
```

Renaming SAS Data Sets

You can rename a disk-format SAS data set with the CHANGE, EXCHANGE, and AGE statements of the DATASETS procedure or with the CMS RENAME command.

SAS Files from Releases 79.6 and 82.3

The internal structure of SAS data sets created under Version 5 of the SAS System is different from the structures used in Releases 79.6 and 82.3. Although Version 5 SAS programs can read and update Release 82.3 SAS data sets and can read Release 79.6 data sets, **you should convert old SAS data sets to Version 5 format.** The Version 5 format uses much less space than the 82.3 format and, therefore, is more efficient.

Converting data sets to Version 5 format can be done with a simple DATA step, such as:

```
DATA newlibref.dataset;
   SET oldlibref.dataset;
```

You can convert an entire library with PROC COPY. For example,

```
PROC COPY IN=oldlibref OUT=newlibref;
```

To convert old SAS data sets to Version 5 format, you must specify a new libref for the converted files. If you specify a libref that matches that of any Release 82.3 or 79.6 data sets, the file or files will not be converted.

Chapter 5

Using External Files in CMS SAS® Programs

INTRODUCTION

In the SAS environment, an *external file* is any file on disk or tape that is not a SAS file. Chapter 3 discusses output and work files, many of which are external files. This chapter discusses external data files. Data stored in external files are usually generated by another program, keyed in with an editor, or created by another data entry technique.

Important note: the CMS SAS System uses the tape-handling facilities of CMS to process tape files. Before you use tape files, be sure to read about tape processing under CMS in the *CMS User's Guide* and the *CMS Command and Macro Reference*.

DCB Characteristics

When reading and writing external files, you may need to consider *DCB characteristics*. DCB characteristics, which specify how data lines (records) are arranged in a file, are *logical record length*, *block size*, and *record format*.

logical record length
LRECL

>specifies the maximum number of bytes in each record. Depending on the record format of a file, LRECL may or may not be equal to the line length or observation length.

block size
BLKSIZE

>specifies the number of bytes per block. Block size is a function of logical record length. (If records are not grouped by blocks, block size is not relevant.) Records do not have to be blocked; however, because disk/tape activity is reduced when records are blocked, it is more efficient to use blocks.
>
>For files in OS-simulated data set format (filemode number 4), the optimal block size contains as many records as possible (as long as the BLKSIZE value does not exceed 32760) without wasting space by filling only part of a large block. For example, if a file has 500 72-byte records and you use a block size of 32760, you waste over 26000 bytes of disk space. Each 32760-byte block can hold 455 72-byte records (455 x 72= 32760), so 45 records of the file must be written in a second block. However, 45 records use only 3240 bytes of the block, leaving 29520 bytes. It is more efficient to use a smaller block size, such as 7200 or 14400. It is not always necessary to calculate the block size with great precision, but you should keep these factors in mind.

record format
RECFM

>specifies whether records are of fixed or variable length, whether or not the file is blocked, and whether or not carriage-control characters are present in column one. Record format is indicated by a combination of one to three characters: F if records are fixed-length, V if records are variable-length, B if records are blocked, S if records are spanned, and A if carriage-control is present. For example, RECFM VBA indicates that the file has variable-length, blocked records with carriage-control characters in column one.

SAS uses default DCB characteristics when reading and writing external files, but these can be overridden by specifying different values on the FILEDEF command or in the INFILE and FILE statements. If you specify DCB options in an INFILE or FILE statement, use an equals sign after the keyword, for example, RECFM=VBA.

Print files (those with carriage-control characters) and *non-print files* (no carriage control) have different default DCB characteristics in SAS programs. Print files have these values:

    LRECL=137
    BLKSIZE=141
    RECFM=VBA

Non-print files have these defaults:

    LRECL=80
    BLKSIZE=6400
    RECFM=FB

If you want to override the default values, you need to know how to calculate LRECL and BLKSIZE. LRECL and BLKSIZE are calculated differently for different record formats.

- When RECFM is FB, LRECL is the length of the longest record, and BLKSIZE is an integer multiple of LRECL. For example, if the longest record is 70 bytes, LRECL is 70, and BLKSIZE is 70 x n, where n is an integer.
- When RECFM is VB, LRECL is the length of the longest record plus four bytes (the additional four bytes contain *record descriptor information*). BLKSIZE is an integer multiple of LRECL plus four (these four bytes contain *block descriptor information*). For example, if the longest data line is 60 bytes long, LRECL is 64, and BLKSIZE is

$$(64 \times n) + 4$$

where n is an integer.
- Any time the RECFM includes an "A" (that is, the file is a print file), add one to the LRECL value to allow for the column containing carriage-control characters.

Consider these examples. To read or write a fixed-length file with a maximum record length of 72 and 100 records per block, specify these values:

```
RECFM FB
LRECL 72
BLKSIZE 7200
```

To read or write a variable-length file with a maximum record length of 200 and 10 records per block, specify these values:

```
RECFM VB
LRECL 204
BLKSIZE 2044
```

To read or write a variable-length **print** file with a maximum record length of 200 and 10 records per block, specify these values:

```
RECFM VBA
LRECL 205
BLKSIZE 2054
```

Note: the maximum allowable line length (not LRECL) for a print file is 255; the default is 132.* To write a file with lines longer than 132 characters in a print file, specify the LINESIZE= option in the FILE statement, as well as the DCB characteristics. For the file above, which has a line length of 200, the FILE statement should be:

```
FILE fileref PRINT LINESIZE=200;
```

---

* The maximum line length you can use depends on the printer you use. Some printers print up to 255 characters, but others do not. Check with installation personnel for the maximum line length of your printer.

READING EXTERNAL FILES

The CMS SAS System can read data stored in CMS disk or tape files, even if they are not SAS files.* External files can be read using the DATA step or by several procedures, such as TAPECOPY, TAPELABEL, and TAPECOMP. The input record length of an external file is limited to 32760 bytes. SAS can read files with fixed- or variable-length data lines and files of mixed record types with almost any arrangement of data values.

The general procedure to read an external file is as follows:

- Issue a CMS FILEDEF command to associate a DDname (also called a *fileref*) with the file to be read.
- In a SAS DATA step, identify the file you want to read by specifying the previously assigned DDname in the SAS INFILE statement. Follow the INFILE statement with one or more INPUT statements that list the variables to be read and describe the arrangement of the input data values. Consult the *SAS User's Guide: Basics, Version 5 Edition* for more information on the INFILE and INPUT statements.
- In a SAS PROC step, specify the DDname (fileref) in the PROC statement.

DCB Characteristics

Under CMS SAS, DCB information must be specified to read external tape files and some external disk files. To specify DCB information, use the options LRECL (logical record length), BLKSIZE (block size), and RECFM (record format) on the FILEDEF command or in the INFILE statement. If you specify incorrect DCB information or if the characteristics of the file are incorrectly marked by CMS, your SAS program may abend or a CMS error message may be issued.

Issuing a CMS FILEDEF Command

The CMS FILEDEF command assigns a DDname (fileref) to the file you want to read. Do not specify any DDnames reserved for use by SAS or CMS. Other names to be avoided are USER, CARDS, WORK, and TAPExxxx, and any name that is the filetype of one of your SAS files.

FILEDEFs to Read Disk Files

The general form of a FILEDEF for a CMS file on disk is

   FILEDEF *DDname* DISK *filename filetype filemode* (*options*

Note: you must specify the actual filename and filetype of an external file. SAS does not substitute names for these parameters as it does for SAS files. The options specified can include DCB information, if needed.

FILEDEFs to Read Tape Files

To read a file from tape, first arrange to have the tape mounted and attached to your virtual machine. Some installations have special commands for tape mounts;

---

* This includes VSAM files (see *SAS Guide to VSAM Processing, Version 5 Edition*) and VM MONITOR files. A disk or tape MONITOR file is referenced by a fileref in the INFILE statement; the RECFM is VB so you must specify DCB attributes to read the records from these devices. A MONITOR file read from the virtual reader is referenced by a fileref followed immediately by the INFILE typeoption keyword MONITOR. Issue a SPOOL RDR HOLD command for the reader file to remain in the virtual reader after processing. Whether reading the file from disk, tape, or the reader, standard INFILE statement options can be specified. MONITOR files are described in IBM's *VM/SP System Programmer's Guide*.

others require that you send a message to the operator. Consult with installation personnel or the local SAS software consultant to find out how to have tapes mounted at your installation.

When the tape is attached to your machine, you receive a message noting the virtual address of the tape drive. Issue a FILEDEF command for the file. The general form of a CMS FILEDEF to read an external file from tape is

FILEDEF *DDname* TAP*n* *labelinfo* (LRECL *n* BLKSIZE *x* RECFM *rf*

Tape label information is for labeled tapes only. The logical record length, block size, and record format are required to read all external tape files. If the DCB information is incorrect, the SAS program abends. (Note: the DCB options can also be specified in the INFILE statement.)

If reading from a nonlabeled tape, use CMS TAPE commands to position the tape immediately following any tapemark that precedes the file to be read. (Positioning tapes with the CMS TAPE commands is reviewed in Chapter 4.) If processing a labeled tape, you do not have to position the tape as long as you specify the correct label information on the FILEDEF command.

SAS INFILE Statement

When you read an external file in a DATA step, the INFILE statement identifies the input data file to SAS. The fileref specified in the INFILE statement must already be associated with the file by a CMS FILEDEF command, as described above. The INFILE statement precedes the INPUT statement to which it applies.

The general form of the SAS INFILE statement is

INFILE *fileref options*;

Consult the *SAS User's Guide: Basics, Version 5 Edition* for a description of the options available in the INFILE statement. INFILE statement options not supported under CMS SAS are listed below:

BSAM
CCHHR=
CLOSE=
DCB=
DEVTYPE=
DSCB=
EOV=
JFCB=
UCBNAME=
VOLUME(S)=
all options for DA, POWER, and VTOC files

Note that members of CMS MACLIBs and TXTLIBs can be accessed with an INFILE statement of the form:

INFILE *fileref* (*member*) *options*;

If your CMS installation supports the access of OS data sets from CMS (shared DASD), you can also read a member of an OS partitioned data set with the *fileref*(*member*) specification. See Appendix 3 for information on accessing OS data sets under the CMS SAS System.

Examples

The sample DATA step below reads a disk-format file and writes the file's contents on the SAS log.

```
CMS FILEDEF INDATA DISK DRUG DOSES A;
DATA _NULL_;
   INFILE INDATA;
   INPUT a1 SUBJECT $7. a9 WEIGHT 3. a13 AGE 2. a16 DOSEDATE DATE7.
         a24 DOSE 3. a28 INITBAC 2.
         a31 CHCKDATE DATE7. a39 BACCNT 2.;
   PUT SUBJECT WEIGHT= AGE= DOSEDATE= DATE7.
       DOSE= INITBAC= CHCKDATE= DATE7. BACCNT=;
RUN;
```

The next example reads a file on a standard-labeled tape and creates a SAS data set from it. The FILEDEF for the tape file includes label and DCB information. Tape positioning commands are not needed because the FILEDEF includes label information.

```
CMS TAPE REW;
CMS FILEDEF MASTER TAP1 SL 3 (LRECL 80 BLKSIZE 6400 RECFM FB;
DATA MALES.GROUP4;
   INFILE MASTER;
   INPUT a1 ID $11. a13 AGE 4.1 a18 SBPR 3. a22 DBPR 3. a26 HRATE 3.;
RUN;
```

WRITING EXTERNAL FILES

The CMS SAS System can also write data to external files on disk or tape. The external files SAS writes are either *print files* (having carriage-control characters in column one) or *non-print* files (no carriage-control characters). Writing external files is similar to reading external files.

- Enter a CMS FILEDEF command to associate a DDname with the file you want to write.
- In a DATA step within a SAS session, identify the file you want to write by specifying the DDname in a SAS FILE statement. Follow the FILE statement with one or more PUT statements. List the variables and character constants to be written, and describe the arrangement of the output data lines in the PUT statement. Consult the *SAS User's Guide: Basics, Version 5 Edition* for more information on the FILE and PUT statements.
- In a PROC step, specify the DDname (fileref) in the PROC statement.

DCB Characteristics

Under CMS SAS, DCB information is necessary to write an external file only if you do not want to use the default values. The defaults are LRECL=137, BLKSIZE=141, and RECFM=VBA for print files; and LRECL=80, BLKSIZE=6400, and RECFM=FB for nonprint files. Specify DCB information on the FILEDEF command or in the FILE statement.

Issuing the CMS FILEDEF Command

The CMS FILEDEF command assigns a DDname to the file you want to write. Do not use DDnames reserved by SAS or CMS, or USER, WORK, CARDS, or TAPExxxx. Also avoid DDnames that duplicate the filetypes of SAS files.

FILEDEFs to Write Disk Files

The general form of a FILEDEF for a CMS disk file is

FILEDEF *DDname* DISK *filename filetype filemode (options*

DCB options can be specified if you want to use characteristics different from the defaults, as described earlier in this chapter.

Usually, SAS starts writing data lines at the beginning of the file. To add data at the end of an existing file, specify the DISP MOD option in the CMS FILEDEF command:

FILEDEF *DDname* DISK *filename filetype filemode* (DISP MOD

FILEDEFs to Write Tape Files

Remember that tape files are easily destroyed by overwriting. Be sure you are familiar with a tape's contents and tape handling under CMS before you write on a tape.

To write a file to tape, first arrange to have the tape mounted with write-access and attached to your virtual machine. Ask installation personnel for assistance if you do not know how to do this. Then issue a FILEDEF command. The general form of a CMS FILEDEF to write an external file to tape is

FILEDEF *DDname* TAP*n labelinfo (options*

Specify tape label information for labeled tapes only. DCB characteristics can be specified if you want to use values other than the SAS defaults.

If writing to a nonlabeled tape, use CMS TAPE commands to position the tape. (Positioning tapes with the CMS TAPE commands is reviewed in Chapter 4.) If processing a labeled tape, you do not have to position the tape as long as you specify the correct label information on the FILEDEF command.

SAS FILE Statement

The FILE statement identifies the output data file. The fileref (DDname) specified in the FILE statement must already be associated with the data file using the CMS FILEDEF command. The FILE statement precedes the PUT statement to which it applies.

The general form of the SAS FILE statement is

FILE *fileref options*;

If you specify the PRINT option in the FILE statement:

`FILE fileref PRINT;`

or use an "A" in the RECFM specification, the file is written as a print file. That is, SAS adds carriage-control characters to the file.

FILE statement options **not supported** under the CMS SAS System are listed below:

CLOSE=
DA
DEVTYPE=
DLI
DSCB=
JFCB=
UCBNAME=
VOLUME=

Examples

Two examples of writing external files follow. In the first example, an external, non-print, disk file is written from a SAS data set. The new file is written with default DCB specifications of LRECL=80, BLKSIZE=6400, and RECFM=FB.

```
CMS FILEDEF OUT DISK SCORES OVER30 A;
DATA _NULL_;
   SET RACE.OVER30;
   FILE OUT;
   PUT NUMBER TIME PLACE;
RUN;
```

The second example demonstrates writing an external file to a nonlabeled tape. The tape is positioned after the third tapemark. DCB characteristics are specified to override the defaults.

```
CMS TAPE REW;
CMS TAPE FSF 3;
CMS FILEDEF WRITE TAP1 (LRECL 40 BLKSIZE 400 RECFM FB;
DATA _NULL_;
   SET CLASS1.TESTS CLASS2.TESTS CLASS3.TESTS;
   FILE WRITE;
   PUT STUDENT T1 T2 T3 T4 T5;
```

Special Files: LOG, PRINT, and PUNCH

You can specify the SAS output files for the log, procedure output, and punch in the FILE statement. If you specify one of these files, lines written with the PUT statement are written to the output file instead of a disk or tape file. To designate one of the output files, use the special fileref LOG, PRINT, or PUNCH in the FILE statement.

Since SAS automatically issues FILEDEFs for the log, procedure output, and punch files, you do not need to issue a FILEDEF as you would to write to a disk or tape file.

Specifying LOG

If you specify

```
FILE LOG options;
```

the lines specified with PUT are written to the SAS log. LOG is the default file for lines written by a PUT statement. If you do not specify a file with a FILE statement, the PUT statement always writes on the SAS log.

As described in Chapter 3, you can direct the SAS log to the terminal, to the virtual printer, or to a CMS disk file with the LTYPE, LPRINT, and LDISK options on the SAS command. When directed to the virtual printer or to a CMS disk file, the LOG file is a print file, and line length is determined by the LINESIZE= option in the SAS FILE statement. If you do not specify the LINESIZE= option in the FILE statement, SAS uses the line length specified by the SAS system option LINESIZE.

When the SAS log is directed to the terminal, it is a non-print file, and the line length is determined by the SAS system option TLINESIZE.

Specifying PRINT

If you specify

```
FILE PRINT options;
```

the lines specified with PUT are printed on pages separate from the log, as is procedure output.

As described in Chapter 3, you can direct the procedure output to the terminal, to the virtual printer, and to a CMS disk file with the PTYPE, PPRINT, and PDISK options on the SAS command. When directed to the virtual printer or to a CMS disk file, PRINT is a print file, and the line length is determined by the LINESIZE= option in the SAS FILE statement. If the LINESIZE= option is not specified in the FILE statement, SAS uses the line length specified by the SAS system option LINESIZE.

When the PRINT file is directed to the terminal, it is a non-print file, and the line length is determined by the SAS system option TLINESIZE.

Specifying PUNCH

If you specify

    FILE PUNCH *options*;

the lines specified with PUT are written to the disk file:

    filename SASPUNCH A

You can specify the filename of the PUNCH file with the NAME option. If the NAME option is not specified, the filename of the first file of SAS source listed on the SAS command is used. If no SAS source file is specified on the SAS command, the PUNCH file is assigned filename SAS. By default, the PUNCH file is a non-print file.

The file can be punched subsequently with the CMS PUNCH command. The PUNCH file is written on the A-disk unless you issue a CMS FILEDEF command to direct the file associated with DDname FT13F001 to another minidisk or to the PUNCH. For example,

    FILEDEF 13 PUNCH (LRECL 80 BLKSIZE 80 RECFM FB

Terminal Files

Data lines can be INPUT from the terminal and PUT to the terminal. To do this, first assign a DDname to the terminal with a CMS FILEDEF command:

    FILEDEF *DDname* TERM

Then specify that DDname in the INFILE and FILE statements.

If the input file is assigned to the terminal, specify the UNBUFFERED option in the INFILE statement:

    INFILE *DDname* UNBUFFERED;

When the input file is assigned to the terminal, use the NULLEOF | NONULLEOF option to determine whether or not a null line signals the end-of-file. If NONULLEOF (the default) is in effect, only a /* or an ENDSAS statement can signal end-of-file. If NULLEOF is in effect, a null line also signals the end-of-file. When NONULLEOF is in effect, the input file should have these DCB characteristics:

LRECL 137
BLKSIZE 141
RECFM VBA

You can specify the DCB characteristics on the FILEDEF command or in the INFILE statement.

Problems sometimes occur if you run an application more than once in a session with INFILE and/or FILE assigned to the terminal. These problems can be avoided if you routinely clear the FILEDEFs for the terminal before executing such an application. Use this FILEDEF form:

```
FILEDEF DDname CLEAR
```

Do not specify an * for the DDname specification.

In the example below, the terminal is used for both input and output. You can use this program to review the contents of a SAS data set. First, the program clears any FILEDEFs that already use the filerefs (DDnames) chosen for the terminal INFILE and FILE. By doing this, you avoid the problems mentioned above. Next, the program issues three FILEDEFs: one for the terminal INFILE (DDname INSCREEN), one for the terminal FILE (DDname OUTSCREE), and one for a file to contain a SAS DATA step (DDname DATASTEP). A PROC CONTENTS step lists the SAS data sets in the DRUG432 SAS data library. Then the program prompts you to enter the name of the data set you want to review; you must specify one of the data sets listed by PROC CONTENTS. The data set name is written to SUBSET SAS as part of a DATA step. Next, the DATA step written to the file SUBSET SAS executes. It creates a temporary SAS data set containing ten observations from the SAS data set named in response to the earlier prompt. Finally, the temporary data set is printed with PROC PRINT.

```
CMS FILEDEF INSCREEN TERM (LRECL 137 BLKSIZE 141 RECFM VBA;
CMS FILEDEF OUTSCREE TERM;
CMS FILEDEF DATASTEP DISK SUBSET SAS A;

PROC CONTENTS DATA=DRUG432._ALL_ NODS;
RUN;

DATA _NULL_;
   IF _N_=2 THEN STOP;
   INFILE INSCREEN UNBUFFERED;
   FILE OUTSCREE;
   PUT 'WHICH DATA SET DO YOU WANT TO SEE?'//
       '(ENTER SAS DATA SET NAME)';
   INPUT DATANAME :$15.;
   FILE DATASTEP;
   PUT 'DATA TEST; SET DRUG432.'@24 DATANAME ' (OBS=10);';
RUN;

%INCLUDE TEMP;
RUN;

PROC PRINT;
RUN;
```

Chapter 6

SAS® System Options

INTRODUCTION

The SAS System has three general categories of options.

- *SAS data set options* are specified in parentheses following a SAS data set's name. These options affect the SAS data set only. RENAME= and KEEP= are examples of SAS data set options. See the "SAS Files" chapter in the *SAS User's Guide: Basics, Version 5 Edition* for descriptions of the SAS data set options.
- *Statement options* are specified in a particular SAS statement, such as the HEADER= option in the FILE statement or an OUT= option in some PROC statements. The action of a statement option affects only the statement or step for which it is specified. Statement options are described in the primary descriptions of the statements to which they apply.
- *SAS system options* are specified in an OPTIONS statement, on the SAS command, or in a PROFILE SAS file. They differ from SAS data set options and statement options because they affect all DATA and PROC steps in a program (unless respecified). For example, the CENTER|NOCENTER option affects all output from a SAS program, regardless of the number of steps in the program. SAS system options control a wide range of operating features, including output destinations and the efficiency of program execution.

This chapter discusses SAS system options only.

TYPES OF SYSTEM OPTIONS

There are two types of SAS system options: on/off options and value options.

On/off options have two possible values. Each value is identified with a keyword, for example, DATE and NODATE.

Value options have many possible settings. Specify these options with an identifying keyword followed by a value. Use an equals sign between the keyword and the value in an OPTIONS statement (for example, LINESIZE=72), but not on the SAS command (LINESIZE 72).

CURRENT OPTION SETTINGS

SAS system options are set to default values. The SAS OPTIONS procedure displays the current settings of the SAS system options on the SAS log. For example,

- `PROC OPTIONS;`   (lists one option per line)
- `PROC OPTIONS SHORT;`   (lists options in compressed format)
- `PROC OPTIONS CMS;`   (lists options for CMS SAS only)

Refer to the *SAS User's Guide: Basics, Version 5 Edition* for more information on PROC OPTIONS.

CHANGING OPTION DEFAULTS

The default values for SAS system options will be appropriate for many of your SAS programs. However, if you need to override one or more default settings, you can do so in one of the following ways:

- Create a file called PROFILE SAS, and specify values for the SAS system options you want to override. (Even though the filetype of this file is SAS, it is not a SAS program. The PROFILE SAS file should contain only option settings, not SAS programming statements.) For example, PROFILE SAS might contain these option specifications:

    CAPS
    CENTER
    DATE
    TLOG

    When you invoke SAS, it searches each accessed minidisk for a PROFILE SAS file, using the standard CMS search order. If a given option is specified in more than one accessed PROFILE SAS file, a setting in the file found earlier in the search order supersedes a setting in a file found later in the search order. For example, there is always a PROFILE SAS file on the SAS System minidisk. If you create a PROFILE SAS on your A-disk as well, it is searched first, and the SAS System minidisk file is searched second. If any options are specified in both files, the setting in PROFILE SAS A supersedes the setting in the other file.
    Note: the combined lengths of options specified in all PROFILE SAS files searched by the SAS System and options specified on the SAS command cannot exceed 100 bytes.
- Specify SAS system options after a left parenthesis in the SAS command:

    `SAS filename (options`

    For on/off options, just list the keyword corresponding to the appropriate setting. For value options, list the keyword identifying the option followed by the value you want to set; do not use an equals sign. For example,

    `SAS (CENTER LINESIZE 72`

- Specify SAS system options in an OPTIONS statement at any point within a SAS session. The options are reset for the duration of the SAS session or until you change them with another OPTIONS statement. The

OPTIONS statement has the form:

OPTIONS *options*;

List the keywords corresponding to the on/off options or *keyword=value* for the value options. For example,

```
OPTIONS CENTER LINESIZE=72;
```

Refer to the *SAS User's Guide: Basics, Version 5 Edition* for more information on the OPTIONS statement.

Important note: some SAS system options have no effect if you specify them in an OPTIONS statement; you must specify them on the SAS command or in PROFILE SAS. **Table 18.3** in the *SAS User's Guide: Basics, Version 5 Edition* indicates those options that you cannot specify in the OPTIONS statement.

When the same option is set in more than one place, the most recent specification is used. The OPTIONS statement takes precedence over the SAS command; the SAS command takes precedence over the PROFILE SAS file; your own PROFILE SAS file takes precedence over the installation defaults.

OPTIONS FOR CMS SAS USERS

The following list is a quick reference to SAS system options that apply only to CMS SAS users. These options are also described in the "SAS System Options" chapter in the *SAS User's Guide: Basics, Version 5 Edition*.

You can specify all of these options in a PROFILE SAS file or on the SAS command. Unless otherwise noted, you cannot specify these options in an OPTIONS statement.

CMDMSG | NOCMDMSG

> specifies whether or not the text of error messages from CMS commands issued from SAS should be displayed at the terminal. The CMDMSG setting is useful in debugging. You can specify this option in an OPTIONS statement.

CMS | NOCMS

> controls whether or not SAS prints the amount of memory and CPU time used for each step on the log. If CMS is in effect, the resource notes are suppressed; NOCMS prints the resource notes.

CPSP | NOCPSP

> determines whether or not the CMS SAS interface issues CP SPOOL commands for the virtual printer. Specify NOCPSP when you are running SAS on a CMS batch machine where spooling commands issued by SAS may interfere with those issued by the CMS batch facility.
>
> If you specify the CPSP and PPRINT options, the CMS SAS interface issues

```
CP SPOOL PRINTER CONT
```

when SAS is invoked and

```
CP SPOOL PRINTER NOCONT CLOSE
```

before returning to CMS at the end of the SAS session. You can specify this option in an OPTIONS statement.

ERASE | NOERASE

> specifies whether or not the SAS WORK files are erased at the beginning and end of a SAS session. If ERASE is in effect, the CMS

SAS interface issues a CMS ERASE command for all files with filetype WORK when a SAS session terminates normally. WORK files are not erased when a SAS session terminates abnormally. Since WORK files might still exist due to an abnormal termination, a CMS ERASE command is also issued at the beginning of a SAS session, before SAS initializes a new WORK library. ERASE is the default.

NOERASE prevents the WORK data sets from being deleted; however, it has no effect on initialization of the WORK data library at the beginning of each session. The initialization process also wipes out existing WORK files. To prevent initialization, specify the SAS system option NOWORKINIT on the SAS command.

You can specify this option in an OPTIONS statement.

FILCLR | NOFILCLR

specifies whether or not SAS issues the command "FILEDEF * CLEAR" during SAS termination. FILCLR clears all FILEDEFs except those issued with the PERM option. When NOFILCLR is in effect, only FILEDEFs issued by SAS are cleared.

FORTG *filename*

names a TXTLIB to be GLOBALed by SAS. You can use this option for user-written procedures or other programs called from within SAS.

NAME *filename*

specifies the filename to be assigned to the disk files for printed procedure output (filetype LISTING), the SAS log (filetype SASLOG), and lines entered at the terminal in interactive mode (filetype SAS).

NULLEOF | NONULLEOF

determines whether or not a null line can be used to signal end-of-file when the input file is assigned to the terminal. NONULLEOF is the default and requires a "/*" or an ENDSAS statement to signal end-of-file. If NULLEOF is in effect, a null line also signals end-of-file.

When NONULLEOF is in effect, the FILEDEF that assigns the INFILE to the terminal must specify these DCB characteristics:

```
LRECL 137 BLKSIZE 141 RECFM VBA
```

PLIO *filename*

names the PL/I optimizing compiler run-time subroutine library on your system. The PLIO option must be specified; at most installations it is included in the SAS System minidisk's PROFILE SAS file.

PSEG *status*

indicates whether or not P-level segments are used when executing SAS programs. A series of SAS software segments can be installed in one or two *overlay levels*. If two levels are installed, the PSEG option determines whether or not the second or P-level segments are used. The values for *status* are SHARED (or ON), NONSHARED, and OFF. See the description of the SSEG option for information on these statuses.

In earlier releases of the SAS System, P-level segments were for SAS procedures. In Version 5, however, this is not the case; procedures are installed in the S-level segments. In Version 5, P-level segments are not typically installed.

You should not change the default setting of this option unless directed to do so by your SAS software consultant.

SASLIB *filename*

directs SAS to issue a CMS GLOBAL command to add the file

> *filename* `TXTLIB` *

to the list of TXTLIBs searched during a SAS session, where *filename* is the name of a TXTLIB containing user-written formats. You need to specify this option only if you are using user-written formats (from PROC FORMAT) that are stored in a TXTLIB.* (See Appendix 2 for information on storing user-written formats.)

SERIES *xy*

specifies which series of segments (DCSS) should be used.** A given series of segments can be installed in one or two levels: S-level segments, which are controlled by the SSEG option, and P-level segments, which are controlled by PSEG. The *x* value identifies the S-level series to use, and *y* identifies the P-level series to use, if any. If only one value is specified and PSEG is in effect, the value identifies the series for both S-level and P-level segments.

SIODISK *filemode*

forces all WORK files from a SAS program or session to be written to the specified minidisk. If you do not specify the SIODISK option, SAS writes WORK files on the write-accessed minidisk with the most available free space when SAS is invoked.

SSEG *status*

determines the use of S-level segments, which contain the SAS supervisor and procedures (procedures were in P-level segments in earlier SAS releases). There are three possible settings for *status*: SHARED (or ON), NONSHARED, and OFF.

- SSEG SHARED or SSEG ON specifies that portions of segments that are shareable are to be shared by CMS SAS users. SSEG SHARED provides the best performance of CMS SAS and the VM system.
- SSEG NONSHARED specifies that shareable portions of segments will not be shared. This specification degrades performance, and you should use it only for special applications.
- SSEG OFF specifies that SAS will not be executed from segments.

You should not change the default setting of this option unless directed to do so by your SAS software consultant.

SVCHND | NOSVCHND

determines if the SAS supervisor call handling is in effect when executing a CMS statement issued from within SAS.

TMSG *level*

determines which messages are typed at the terminal when the SAS log is not directed to the terminal.

- TMSG NOTES specifies that all notes and errors be typed.
- TMSG ERRORS specifies that only error messages be typed. This is the default.

---

* Under Release 82.3 of the SAS System, the SASLIB option caused a FILEDEF to be issued for the TXTLIB. Under Version 5 this FILEDEF is not issued. This affects your programs only if you use the SUGI supplemental library procedure FMTLIB.

** Installing and using SAS software from segments significantly reduces memory requirements for SAS programs. If you need more information on saving SAS in segments, see SAS Technical Report Y-105.

• TMSG OFF specifies that no messages be typed.

You can specify this option in an OPTIONS statement.

TXTLIB | NOTXTLIB

determines whether or not text libraries included in a CMS GLOBAL TXTLIB specification before SAS is invoked are searched during a SAS session. If you specify TXTLIB, any text libraries included in a CMS GLOBAL TXTLIB specification before SAS is invoked are added to the end of the list of libraries searched during a SAS session.

With either setting of this option, the list of global text libraries is returned to its pre-SAS status at the end of the SAS session. (The NOTXTLIB setting is more efficient than TXTLIB.)

VIOBUF *n*K

specifies the maximum size (in kilobytes) of virtual I/O storage allocated for the SAS WORK library. VIOBUF= does not allocate a fixed amount of space; instead, it sets a limit on the amount of space. To force all WORK files to be written to disk, specify VIOBUF 0.

ZEROMEM | NOZEROMEM

controls whether or not all memory is set to binary zeros. This option is for diagnostic use only and should be used only when requested by SAS Institute Technical Support staff. You can specify this option in an OPTIONS statement.

Chapter 7

Memory and Space Requirements

MEMORY REQUIREMENTS

The amount of memory (virtual storage) needed to run a CMS SAS program or session depends upon a number of factors, including:

- whether or not SAS software is installed in DisContiguous Saved Segments (DCSS)*
- whether or not you are using display manager
- whether or not you are using the SAS macro language
- the procedure being executed
- the number of variables being analyzed
- the number of levels for classification variables
- the statistics requested
- the number of observations in a SAS data set.

It is possible to establish general guidelines for memory requirements:

- If SAS software is **not executed** from segments, DATA steps and most PROC steps run in a 3000K (3M) virtual machine. The CHART, PLOT, FREQ, ANOVA, and GLM procedures usually require a 4000K (4M) virtual machine, and the SAS/AF, SAS/ETS, SAS/FSP, SAS/IML, and SAS/OR software products also require a 4M machine.
- If SAS software is run in segments, memory requirements are typically 1500K (1.5M) for DATA steps and all procedures and software products. This represents a significant reduction in resource usage. If you use display manager, an additional 600K of memory is required.

To find out if you are running SAS in segments, execute PROC OPTIONS, and check the value of the SSEG option. If SSEG is SHARED, ON, or NONSHARED, then segments are being used.

---

* Your installation can install some or all SAS software in segments. See SAS Technical Report Y-105 if you need information on saving segments.

Insufficient Memory

You can encounter three basic memory problems:

1. There may be insufficient memory to load a procedure.
2. Even if a procedure can be loaded, there may not be enough memory allocated to the procedure to complete execution.
3. Memory may be fragmented rather than contiguous.

Insufficient memory can result in abnormal termination of your SAS session. Often an error message is issued that indicates what the problem is. However, sometimes there is not enough memory for the system to determine the nature of the problem, and therefore, no error message is issued.

Insufficient Memory to Load a Procedure

If there is not enough memory to load a SAS procedure, the SAS session usually terminates abnormally (abends), and a CMS error message may be issued, such as:

```
INSUFFICIENT VIRTUAL STORAGE CAPACITY FOR SAS MODULE
TRY DEFINING STORAGE TO nM
```

If there is not enough memory to load a SAS procedure or CMS SAS library routines, you need a bigger virtual machine. Before increasing virtual storage, determine the size of the current virtual machine by issuing a QUERY STORAGE command. The system responds with the size of your virtual machine.

To increase the size of your virtual machine, issue the CP command DEFINE STORAGE, specifying the number of bytes of memory you want for your virtual machine. For example,

```
DEFINE STORAGE 1500K
```

Defining a new machine size terminates your CMS session, and you return to CP. At some installations, CMS is automatically loaded after you define a new machine size. If this is not the case at your installation, use the CP command IPL to invoke CMS again. For example,

```
IPL CMS
```

Insufficient Memory to Execute a Procedure

The SAS System can also run out of memory during the execution of a procedure. When this happens, the PROC step terminates, but the SAS session usually continues. An error message is issued.

Insufficient memory to execute a procedure may indicate that the SAS System did not allocate enough memory for the procedure, or it may indicate that your virtual machine is too small for that particular program. Try one of these measures to solve the problem:

- Reinvoke SAS and specify VIOBUF 0. This forces the entire WORK data library to disk and frees up a small amount of additional memory. You cannot specify VIOBUF in an OPTIONS statement in the middle of a SAS session.
- Increase the size of your virtual machine by 1M.

You should try specifying VIOBUF 0 first. If this does not help, try increasing the size of the virtual machine.

Fragmented Memory

CMS SAS programs require contiguous storage, that is, one continuous area of memory. If the available memory is broken into multiple small areas (fragmented memory), the safest procedure is to end the SAS session, issue the IPL CMS command, and reinvoke SAS.

Factors That Affect General Memory Requirements

If you are concerned about memory usage, here are a number of considerations to keep in mind:

- Do not invoke CMS SAS under IBM's ISPF, DMS, or similar facilities. If you do, memory must be available for both CMS SAS and the facility. More than 3M memory may be required if you run SAS under these circumstances.
- In general, memory requirements are reduced significantly if you execute SAS without display manager and/or the macro facility (that is, by running with NODMS and/or NOMACRO in effect). You can also reduce CPU and I/O requirements if SPOOL, INCLUDE, CHKPOINT, and/or GRAPHICS are not in effect (that is, by using NOSPOOL, NOINCLUDE, NOCHKPOINT, and/or NOGRAPHICS).
- If SAS software is installed in segments, use them. Segments are available to you if SSEG SHARED, SSEG ON, or SSEG NONSHARED is in effect.
- Approximately 64 bytes are needed for the file-id of each file on each accessed minidisk, even if the files are not used in the SAS program. For example, if you access a minidisk with 100 files on it, at least 6400 bytes of memory are required just for the file-ids on that disk. Accessing multiple minidisks containing many files can lead to fragmented memory.
- Each member of a GLOBALed TXTLIB requires at least 32 bytes of memory; this figure can become significant if many large TXTLIBs are GLOBALed. This is not a matter of concern to most users; however, some installations have modified their systems to GLOBAL several TXTLIBs automatically. If this is the case at your installation and it causes you to run out of storage regularly, use the CMS SAS option NOTXTLIB so that only TXTLIBs required for a SAS program are used.
- If segments containing CMS overlap your virtual machine's address space, some of the memory to which you have access is taken up by CMS. This problem is not easy for a user to diagnose and must be solved by installation personnel (for example, the local SAS software representative).
- Each SAS data set referenced in a SAS program requires at least n bytes of memory, where n is the block size of the data set. Therefore, a small SAS data set with a large block size wastes memory. This is one reason why you should be careful to specify an optimal block size for permanent SAS data sets.
- By default, the amount of memory allocated for the WORK files in a SAS program is a function of the size of your virtual machine. However, the CMS SAS option VIOBUF overrides the default. VIOBUF specifies how many 8K buffers of memory are used for the SAS WORK data library. For example, if you specify VIOBUF 10, 80K are needed just for the WORK library in a SAS job. Do not specify a large value for VIOBUF unless it is really necessary.

RUNNING OUT OF SPACE

A SAS program may generate a very large file that uses up all of the available space on a CMS minidisk.

- If a SAS file is being written and you are using display manager or line-mode execution, messages similar to these appear on your terminal:

```
DMSERD107S DISK 'B(0192)' IS FULL.
CLEAR SPACE AND ISSUE 'RETURN' TO CONTINUE PROCESSING
CMS SUBSET
```

The first message tells you which minidisk is full; in this example, the B-disk, at virtual address 192, is the full minidisk. The second and third messages tell you that CMS SAS has temporarily suspended its processing and has placed your session in CMS subset mode. In the CMS subset, you have the opportunity to remove files from the minidisk and make room for the file being created. You can use the LISTFILE and FILELIST commands to see what files are on the minidisk, and you can use the ERASE command to get rid of unnecessary files. (Do not erase any WORK files because SAS may need them to complete the program.) You cannot use the COPYFILE command in CMS subset mode, but you can use XEDIT to copy a file to another minidisk before erasing the file. Enter the RETURN command when you are ready to resume execution of CMS SAS.

If you cannot clear any space on the minidisk, CMS SAS will terminate abnormally after you enter the RETURN command.

- If a SAS file is being written in noninteractive or batch mode or if an external file is being written, CMS SAS terminates abnormally, and you receive messages similar to the following:

```
DMSERD107S DISK 'A(0191)' IS FULL.
DMSSCT120S OUTPUT ERROR 013 ON FT11F001.
DMSABN148T SYSTEM ABEND 001 CALLED FROM F25E18.
CMS
```

The first message indicates which minidisk filled up (in this case, the A-disk). The second message gives the DDname of the file that was being written at the time of the abend (here, FT11F001, the SAS log). The third message gives the abend code, and the fourth message indicates that you have returned to a CMS session. Notice that the message says CMS rather than CMS SUBSET. When you get the CMS SUBSET message, you know you can recover the file, but when the message is CMS, it cannot be recovered.

If you want to rerun the program that caused the abend, be sure you direct the file to another minidisk, a temporary disk, or tape, depending on the kind of file and whether it is permanent or temporary. You can use a FILEDEF command to specify where the file should be written.

Glossary

The following list defines a variety of terms as they are used in this book.

attention interrupt
> a signal to the system that you issue in order to interrupt processing.

batch
> a mode of execution in which all processing is done in a CMS batch machine. This is **not** the same as the SAS System's *noninteractive mode*, which executes in your virtual machine. Also, you should not confuse batch execution with the SAS system option BATCH, which indicates noninteractive execution.

block size
> an attribute of a file that indicates the number of bytes in a block. If records in a file are grouped by block (blocked), block size is usually a function of logical record length. If records are not grouped by blocks, block size is not relevant. Records in a file do not have to be blocked; however, because disk/tape activity is reduced when records are blocked, it is more efficient to use blocks.

buffer
> an area in the computer's memory containing a block of data that are being read or written.

carriage-control characters
> characters that control line skipping and page ejects when a file is printed. These characters are usually in column one of the records in the file. Not all files contain carriage-control characters; those that do are called *print files*.

catalog
> one of several types of SAS files. A SAS catalog contains entries consisting of screens, function key definitions, letters, and so on. The SAS catalog is used primarily with SAS/FSP, SAS/AF, and SAS/GRAPH software, although function key definitions are used in base SAS software's display manager system.

CMS
> a component of the VM operating system that provides many of the facilities you use at your terminal, such as editing and file management. CMS stands for "Conversational Monitor System."

control language
> a term that refers to CP and CMS commands. Use control language to communicate with the VM operating system, just as you use SAS statements to communicate with the SAS System.

CP
> a part of the VM system that manages hardware devices (for example, the terminal and disks). The CMS component of VM depends on CP for certain services, such as connecting to other users' disks or defining the amount of memory for your virtual machine. CP stands for "Control Program."

data set
>   a term often used as a synonym for *file*. In SAS programming, a SAS
>   data set is a particular kind of SAS file. Not all SAS files are SAS data
>   sets. (See also SAS data set.)

DCB characteristics
>   information that describes the structure of a file. The DCB (Data
>   Control Block) characteristics are logical record length, block size,
>   and record format.

DDname
>   a word associated with a specific file by a CMS FILEDEF command.
>   The CMS DDname corresponds to a SAS libref, which you use in
>   SAS statements to reference a SAS file or files. The DDname also
>   corresponds to a SAS fileref, which you use in SAS statements to
>   reference external (non-SAS) files.

disk
>   a device for data storage that allows direct access to any record. Disk
>   storage differs from tape and card storage, which allow only
>   sequential processing of records.

display manager system
>   a facility of the SAS System for interactive program execution.
>   Display manager consists of three screens for program development
>   and output display, and it uses a number of specialized commands
>   and function keys.

editor
>   a facility for creating and updating disk files.

EXEC
>   a CMS file containing CMS and CP commands and other statements.
>   You execute all of the commands in the EXEC file by issuing one
>   EXEC command or implied EXEC command. An EXEC file is a
>   convenient way to store sequences of commands that you use
>   frequently because you need only one command (the EXEC
>   command) to execute them.

external file
>   any file that is **not** a SAS file. External files can contain data, text, the
>   SAS log, SAS programming statements, or anything else.

file
>   a collection of information (data, text, programming statements, and
>   so on) that CMS handles as a discrete entity. A permanent file is one
>   stored on disk or tape; a temporary file exists only for the duration of
>   a program or a session.

file-id
>   the complete name of a CMS file, composed of the *filename*, *filetype*,
>   and *filemode*.

filemode
>   a letter/number combination given to each CMS file. The letter
>   identifies the minidisk on which a file resides. The number (from 0-6)
>   assigns the file to a certain category. Filemode 0 means the file can
>   only be accessed if its disk is accessed in read/write mode. Most
>   files have filemode number 1, which is an unrestricted category.
>   Filemode 2 indicates a file that is shared by many users; 3 indicates
>   that the file is to be erased as soon as it is read; 4 indicates the file is

in OS simulated data set format; 5 indicates no restrictions but can be used to group files you want to handle together; 6 indicates "update in place" (applicable only for certain kinds of disk files). The filemode is the last parameter of a CMS file-id.

filename

the first parameter of the three-part file-id of a CMS file. The second-level name of a SAS file corresponds to the CMS filename.

fileref

a word used in SAS programming statements (such as INFILE and FILE) that references an external file. The fileref has a function similar to that of the libref, which is for a SAS file. A fileref corresponds to the DDname assigned to the external file by the FILEDEF for that file.

filetype

the second parameter of the three-part file-id of a CMS file. Certain filetypes are used for particular kinds of files; for example, SAS is used as the filetype for files containing SAS programming statements. The libref of a SAS file corresponds to the CMS filetype.

graphics catalog

a type of SAS file containing entries that are graphs produced by SAS/GRAPH software.

interactive execution

the type of execution that occurs when programs are run in your virtual machine. There are three subsets of interactive execution for SAS programs: display manager, line-mode, and noninteractive.

libref

a word that references one or more SAS files in a SAS data library. The libref is the first-level name of a SAS file. It corresponds to the CMS filetype and to the DDname assigned to a file with a FILEDEF command.

line-mode execution

a type of interactive SAS execution in which you enter statements at a terminal in response to prompts from the SAS System. SAS executes steps and displays the output at the terminal by default.

logical record length

the maximum number of bytes in each record in a file. Depending on the record format of a file, logical record length may or may not be equal to the line length or observation length.

model file

a type of SAS file that contains a model produced with SAS/ETS software.

noninteractive

a type of interactive SAS execution in which you execute a SAS program stored in a CMS file by naming the file in the SAS command. There is no prompting, and once the statements stored in the file have executed, SAS terminates. This is not the same as *batch execution*, which executes in a CMS batch machine.

OS

the family of OS/VS1, MVS, VSP, OS/SP and related operating systems.

output files
> files containing information generated from SAS programs. The SAS log and SAS procedure output are output files. These may be written to the terminal, to a disk or tape file, or to a printer, depending on the options you choose.

read access
> the ability to read files, but not to write them.

record format
> a term that refers to whether records in a file are of fixed or variable length, whether or not the file is blocked, and whether or not carriage-control characters are present in column one. Record format is indicated by a combination of one to three characters: F if records are fixed-length, V if records are variable-length, B if records are blocked, S if records are spanned, and A if carriage-control is present. For example, record format VBA indicates that the file has variable-length, blocked records with carriage-control characters in column one.

RSCS
> a component of VM that handles files sent to remote devices (such as a printer). RSCS stands for Remote Spooling Communications Subsystem.

SAS data set
> a specially structured collection of data produced by a SAS DATA step or procedure. A SAS data set is one of several types of SAS files.

SAS file
> a specially structured file created by and processed by the SAS System. SAS data sets, catalogs, graphics catalogs, model files, and saved work space files are all kinds of SAS files.

SAS/IML work space
> a type of SAS file containing saved work space from a SAS/IML session.

source file
> a file containing SAS programming statements.

subset mode
> a special CMS environment in which only certain CMS and CP commands can be used. In subset mode any CP or CMS command that does not alter your virtual storage can be issued. For example, you can use the LINK command in subset mode, but not the COPYFILE command. Under CMS, you enter subset mode from the CMS editor environment, using the editing subcommand CMS. Under SAS, subset mode is invoked with the statement:

> ```
> CMS;
> ```

virtual devices
> a term that refers to the simulated equivalents of real hardware devices. Your *virtual machine* simulates a real computer. You communicate with your virtual machine the way a computer operator communicates with a real computer. A computer operator controls the real computer from an operator's console; your terminal is your *virtual console*. Your virtual machine is connected to *virtual disks* (*minidisks*), which simulate a real disk pack. Similarly, your *virtual printer* is not an actual printer. It is a device to which you

send files that you want to print. The files are routed from your virtual printer to a real printer when one is available. Whenever you see the word *virtual,* remember that it means simulated.

write access

a term that refers to the ability to write or modify files, as well as to read them.

User-written Formats

Creating and Storing Formats
Combining Formats in TXTLIBs

Creating and Storing Formats

You can create your own formats for printing variable values with the FORMAT procedure. You can also store these formats on disk so that they are available for repeated use.

Under the CMS SAS System, all user-written formats are written to loose TEXT files, whether they are temporary or permanent formats.

To create temporary formats, **do not** specify the LIBRARY= option in the PROC FORMAT statement. When SAS executes a PROC FORMAT statement without the LIBRARY= option, the formats created are temporary and are erased at the end of the SAS session.

To create permanent formats, specify LIBRARY=LIBRARY in the PROC FORMAT statement. The format's name becomes the TEXT file's filename. For example, when this PROC FORMAT step executes:

```
PROC FORMAT LIBRARY=LIBRARY;
    VALUE VOTER 1='DEMOCRAT'...;
```

a permanent file is created with filename VOTER and filetype TEXT. This TEXT file is not erased at the end of the SAS session. (You can specify any value for LIBRARY=, but we recommend LIBRARY.)

Note: the default disk for TEXT files is the write-access minidisk with the most available space, usually your A-disk. To store a format TEXT file on another disk, issue a FILEDEF that specifies LIBRARY as the DDname and the filemode of your choice. You can specify dummy values for filename and filetype.

To read existing user-written formats, simply name the format in the appropriate SAS statement. When SAS determines that the format is not a standard SAS format, it looks for a TEXT file with a matching filename. If no TEXT file is found, SAS searches all GLOBALed TXTLIBs to find the format.

Combining Formats in TXTLIBs

If you choose to do so, you can use the CMS TXTLIB command to bundle TEXT files containing formats into one TXTLIB. SAS can read formats that are stored in a TXTLIB, but it will not write formats directly to a TXTLIB.

If you move permanent formats to a TXTLIB, the TXTLIB must be GLOBALed in order to use the formats. Either issue a CMS GLOBAL command yourself, or specify the SASLIB option on the SAS command. For example,

```
SAS (SASLIB filename
```

where *filename* is the filename of the TXTLIB containing the formats. When the SASLIB option appears, SAS issues a GLOBAL command for the TXTLIB with the specified filename. This makes the TXTLIB available for searching.

Cross-System Compatibility

INTRODUCTION

This appendix discusses file compatibility between the CMS SAS System and the SAS System running under other operating systems. Three different situations are addressed:

- accessing SAS files created under the CMS SAS System from other operating systems
- accessing SAS files created under another operating system, using the CMS SAS System
- accessing external files created under another operating system, using the CMS SAS System.

SAS FILES CREATED UNDER CMS

Tape Files

Access from OS or VSE Systems

You can use an OS SAS or a VSE SAS System to access any CMS SAS file on tape without having to reformat the file in any way. If you are an OS SAS or a VSE

SAS user, be aware that CMS tapes are usually nonlabeled, so you should use the appropriate parameters in control language when accessing tapes written under CMS.

Access from AOS/VS, PRIMOS, or VMS Systems

You can use the SAS System running under the AOS/VS, PRIMOS, or VMS operating systems to access SAS data sets and catalogs on tape. However, you cannot access graphics catalogs, work space files, and model files. The SAS data set or catalog **must be in transport format** before it can be accessed by the other system.

You can change a SAS data set from standard SAS format to transport format by using PROC XCOPY in CMS SAS. After XCOPY writes the SAS data set(s) to tape in transport format, the data set(s) should be read under AOS/VS, PRIMOS, or VMS with PROC COPY (specifying the IMPORT option) or with a DATA step (specifying the TRANSPORT= option).

You can change a SAS catalog from standard SAS format to transport format using PROC CPORT in CMS SAS. After CPORT writes the catalog to tape in transport format, the catalog should be read under AOS/VS, PRIMOS, or VMS with PROC CIMPORT. Note that CPORT and CIMPORT are available only with SAS/AF software.

Disk Files

Access from VM/PC Systems

When the VM/PC remote server program, VMPCSERV, is active, you can access CMS minidisks on a mainframe from a VM/PC session. Therefore, you can access CMS SAS files for reading or writing from a VM/PC SAS session. The files should be in standard SAS format, not transport format.

Access from AOS/VS, OS, PRIMOS, VMS, or VSE Systems

You cannot use any of these operating systems to access CMS SAS files on disk.

SAS FILES CREATED UNDER OTHER SYSTEMS

Tape Files

Created by OS or VSE Systems

You can use CMS SAS to process an OS SAS or VSE SAS file on tape. If the tape has standard labels, use the SL option in the FILEDEF for the tape, or use CMS TAPE command options to bypass the labels and treat the tape as nonlabeled. You can copy the OS SAS or VSE SAS file to a CMS minidisk with PROC COPY or leave the file on the tape.

Created by AOS/VS, PRIMOS, or VMS Systems

The CMS SAS System can access tape SAS data sets created by the SAS System running under the AOS/VS, PRIMOS, or VMS operating systems. However, CMS SAS cannot access catalogs, graphics catalogs, work space files, and model files. The SAS data set **must be in transport format** to be accessed by the CMS SAS System. To write a transport-format SAS data set in one of these environments, use the TRANSPORT= data set option in a DATA step, or use the EXPORT option in a PROC COPY statement. Then read the transport format data set under CMS SAS with PROC XCOPY.

Disk Files

Created by OS or VSE Systems

If your installation supports *shared DASD* (that is, if you can read OS or VSE disks from CMS), you can use CMS SAS to read a disk-format OS SAS file or VSE SAS file (unless the VSE SAS file is on an FBA disk).

To read an OS or VSE SAS file, first use the CMS commands LINK and ACCESS to access the appropriate disk. Then issue a FILEDEF to define the file to CMS SAS. For example,

```
LINK userid vaa1 vaa2 RR
ACCESS vaa2 fm
FILEDEF DDname filemode DSN file-id
```

The userid and virtual address parameters for the OS or VSE disk in the LINK and ACCESS commands are site-dependent; someone at your computer installation can tell you what values to specify. Once you have accessed the disk and defined the file, you can proceed with your SAS job.

You cannot write to an OS or VSE disk SAS data library from CMS SAS.

Created by AOS/VS, PRIMOS, VM/PC, or VMS Systems

You cannot use CMS SAS to access SAS files on disk created by these systems.

EXTERNAL FILES CREATED UNDER OTHER SYSTEMS

Tape Files

Created by OS or VSE Systems

You can use CMS SAS to read OS and VSE external files on tape with INFILE and INPUT statements, just as you would for CMS external files. Remember that if the OS or VSE tape is standard-labeled, you should specify the SL option in the FILEDEF command or position the tape to bypass any labels.

Created by AOS/VS, PRIMOS, or VMS Systems

You cannot access external files created by these systems with CMS SAS.

Disk Files

Created by OS Systems

If your installation supports shared DASD (that is, if you can read OS files from CMS), you can read most external OS disk files with the CMS SAS System. An exception to this is a VBS file with logical record length greater than 32K. You cannot write to an OS disk from a CMS SAS program.

Created by VSE Systems

If your installation supports shared DASD from CMS to VSE (that is, if you can read VSE files from CMS), you can also read most external VSE files unless the VSE file is on an FBA disk. You cannot write to a VSE disk from a CMS SAS program.

EXECs in CMS SAS® Programs

INTRODUCTION

CMS EXEC files can be very useful in CMS SAS programming. This appendix shows an example using the CMS EXEC language for a SAS application. This appendix also describes a function and a CALL routine you can use to transfer information between the SAS System and EXECs written in EXEC 2 or REXX.

If you are not familiar with the CMS EXEC languages (EXEC, EXEC 2, and REXX) and want to learn about them, see these IBM publications:

CMS User's Guide
CMS Command and Macro Reference
EXEC 2 Reference
System Product Interpreter Reference
System Product Interpreter User's Guide.

Note that you can also use the SAS macro language for many of the applications for which you might use an EXEC.

EXAMPLE

The EXEC languages are useful for executing SAS programs that are almost, but not quite, alike. For example, the file AGRI SAS (shown below) is a SAS program that creates a SAS data set containing data on agricultural production. The data are read from external files that are divided by state. In the AGRI SAS file, the string " QQQ " appears wherever a state name should be inserted.

```
CMS FILEDEF DATAIN DISK CORN  QQQ ;
DATA CORN;
   INFILE DATAIN;
   INPUT COUNTY CYIELD CACRES;
   TITLE 'SOYBEAN YIELD VS CORN YIELD FOR THE STATE OF  QQQ ';
RUN;
CMS FILEDEF DATAIN DISK SOY  QQQ ;
DATA SOY;
   INFILE DATAIN;
```

```
      INPUT COUNTY SYIELD SACRES;
  RUN;
  DATA    QQQ .MERGECS;
      MERGE CORN SOY;
      BY COUNTY;
  RUN;
  PROC PLOT;
      PLOT SYIELD * CYIELD;
  RUN;
```

The AGRI SAS program can be executed by the following EXEC, called AGRI EXEC:

```
  &TRACE
  &IF &INDEX = 0 &GOTO -MSG
  &STACK TOP
  &STACK C /  QQQ  / &1 / * *
  &STACK FFILE CSNEW
  XEDIT AGRI SAS
  EXEC SAS CSNEW (LT LD
  &EXIT
  -MSG
  &TYPE PLEASE SPECIFY STATE NAME (LIMIT OF 8 CHARACTERS)
  &EXIT
```

AGRI EXEC uses XEDIT to change every occurrence of " QQQ " in AGRI SAS to a specified state name. You can specify a state name when the EXEC is invoked. For example,

```
  AGRI OHIO
```

If you do not specify a state name when the EXEC is invoked, the EXEC prompts you for the state name. The EXEC then invokes SAS using a second EXEC.

When AGRI EXEC is invoked with OHIO as the state name, this SAS program is executed:

```
  CMS FILEDEF DATAIN DISK CORN  OHIO ;
  DATA CORN;
      INFILE DATAIN;
      INPUT  COUNTY CYIELD CACRES;
      TITLE 'SOYBEAN YIELD VS CORN YIELD FOR THE STATE OF  OHIO ';
  RUN;
  CMS FILEDEF DATAIN DISK SOY  OHIO ;
  DATA SOY;
      INFILE DATAIN;
      INPUT COUNTY SYIELD SACRES;
  RUN;
  DATA  OHIO .MERGECS;
      MERGE CORN SOY;
      BY COUNTY;
  RUN;
  PROC PLOT;
      PLOT SYIELD * CYIELD;
  RUN;
```

GETEXEC AND PUTEXEC

GETEXEC Function

The GETEXEC function is a SAS DATA step function that returns the value of an EXEC variable. The EXEC must be written in EXEC 2 or REXX. The form of the function is

GETEXEC('*argument*')

where *argument* is the name of the EXEC variable. For example, the statement

```
DISKID = GETEXEC('LABEL');
```

assigns the value of the EXEC variable &LABEL to the SAS variable DISKID.

If an EXEC 2 variable name used as an argument to GETEXEC does not exist or has a null value, GETEXEC returns a missing value. (In REXX the value of a variable that has not been used is its name.)

PUTEXEC CALL Routine

The PUTEXEC CALL statement routine assigns a value to an EXEC variable. The EXEC must be written in EXEC 2 or REXX. The form of the routine is

CALL PUTEXEC('*argument1*',*argument2*);

where *argument1* is the name of an EXEC variable and *argument2* is the value to be assigned. Argument1 must be enclosed in single quotes. Argument2 can be specified as a literal or a variable name. If you specify a literal, it must be enclosed in single quotes. For example, the statement:

```
CALL PUTEXEC('LABEL','USR191');
```

specifies the literal USR191 as the value to assign to the EXEC variable &LABEL.

If the variable you specify as *argument1* does not currently exist as an EXEC variable, it will be created.

Usage Notes

Here are some points to keep in mind when using GETEXEC and PUTEXEC:

- All EXEC variable names specified as arguments for GETEXEC and PUTEXEC **must be in uppercase**. This is true for REXX as well as EXEC 2, even though REXX makes no distinction between upper- and lowercase in its variable names. If you specify a REXX compound symbol, such as NAME.1, as an argument, only the stem (the part of the name preceding the period) must be in uppercase.
- Although EXEC 2 variables always begin with an ampersand (&), you must omit the ampersand when you use the name as an argument (see the examples above).
- The CMS EXEC processor hides all variables except those in the "current" EXEC. Hidden variables are not accessible by GETEXEC and PUTEXEC. For example, the variable FILEID in the following sample from an EXEC:

```
FILEID = "MYDATA FILE A1"
'EXEC SAS PROGRAM1'
EXIT
```

is not accessible by GETEXEC because the execution of SAS EXEC hides the variables.
- Arguments to GETEXEC and PUTEXEC must be character values, and the

values of EXEC variables, even numeric values, are always retained in character format. By default, the SAS System converts values automatically from numeric to character or character to numeric. However, it is better to use the DATA step functions INPUT and PUT to convert character values from EXEC variables to a specific numeric format, and vice versa.

- If the interface to EXEC variables fails for some reason, GETEXEC and PUTEXEC assume that all their arguments are invalid (because no EXEC variables can accessed), and a message is written to the SAS log.

Sample Application

Using the SAS EXEC as an example, you can see possible applications for GETEXEC and PUTEXEC. In Version 5 of the SAS System the SAS command is implemented by using an EXEC written in EXEC 2. You can modify the SAS EXEC to set variable values, which can then be accessed and modified in a DATA step. For instance, the SAS EXEC could be modified to provide the label of a user's A-disk:

```
&TRACE
QUERY DISK A (LIFO          <-- add this
&READ VARS &LABEL *         <-- add this
&READ VARS                  <-- add this
...original EXEC statements...
&COMMAND SAS &ARGSTRING
...original EXEC statements...
&EXIT &SRC
```

When the EXEC is modified as shown, you can retrieve the value of &LABEL with GETEXEC.

You can also use PUTEXEC to assign a value to an EXEC variable in the SAS EXEC. For example, suppose the SAS EXEC is further modified as follows:

```
&COMMAND SAS &ARGSTRING
...original EXEC statements...
&TYPE &OBS OBS HAVE BEEN PROCESSED.   <-- add this
&EXIT &SRC
```

A SAS program can set the value of &OBS with statements such as these:

```
DATA TWO;
  LENGTH CN $6;
  SET ONE END=ALLDONE;
  ...more SAS statements...
  IF (ALLDONE) THEN DO;
     CN = PUT(_N_, $6.);
     CALL PUTEXEC('OBS', CN);
  END;
RUN;
```

The TAPECOMP
Procedure

ABSTRACT

The TAPECOMP procedure compares tape files byte by byte.

INTRODUCTION

PROC TAPECOMP compares files on two tapes. The procedure operates on physical files, counting tapemarks to determine where new files begin. Labels are considered to be files and, as such, are not processed as labels, but they are compared in the same way as other data on the tape. The procedure's output lists the number of differences detected between the files.

Before you invoke PROC TAPECOMP, have the tapes you want to compare mounted. Consult installation personnel if you do not know how to have a tape mounted. Be sure you know which drives the tapes are mounted on before you execute TAPECOMP.

Once the tapes are mounted, it is a good idea to issue a TAPE REW command to ensure that the tape has been rewound and is positioned at the beginning. If you are not familiar with CMS TAPE command specifications for tape positioning, refer to Chapter 4, "CMS SAS Files," for a summary. Also see IBM's *CMS Command and Macro Reference* for the primary description of the TAPE command.

SPECIFICATIONS

The only statement used with this procedure is the PROC statement.

   PROC TAPECOMP *options*;

PROC TAPECOMP Statement

   PROC TAPECOMP *options*;

You can specify the following options:

DETACHALL

   causes TAPECOMP to issue a CP DETACH command for each of the tapes after the comparison is complete.

FSF=*n*

>   tells TAPECOMP to forward-space *n* tapemarks before the
>   comparison begins.

LOG

>   specifies that the output from the procedure should be written to the
>   SAS log rather than to the procedure output file.

MAXFILES=*n*

>   specifies the maximum number of files to compare. For example, if
>   you specify MAXFILES=3, three files on each tape are compared. If
>   you do not specify MAXFILES=, the procedure will compare all files
>   on the tapes until end-of-tape is reached on one of the tapes.

TAP*n*

>   specifies the tape drives to be used for the comparison. For example,
>   if the tapes you want to compare have been mounted on drives 183
>   and 184, you would specify TAP3 and TAP4. If you do not specify
>   TAP*n*, the default drives are 181 (TAP1) and 182 (TAP2).

DETAILS

Printed Output

The TAPECOMP procedure's output is divided into INDIVIDUAL FILE REPORTs,
one for each pair of files compared, and a SUMMARY REPORT, which is a sum-
mation of the information in the INDIVIDUAL FILE REPORTs.

An INDIVIDUAL FILE REPORT includes the following information for each
tape:

1. DENSITY OF TAP*n*, the tape density (bytes per inch)
2. FILENO, the number of the file on the tape
3. MINBLOCK, the smallest block size in the file
4. MAXBLOCK, the largest block size in the file
5. #BLOCKS, the number of blocks in the file.

Two other values are reported in a FILE REPORT:

6. LENGTH-ERRORS, the number of records in the files for which record
   lengths differed
7. DATA-ERRORS, the number of records in the files for which the data
   differed.

The SUMMARY REPORT gives the smallest MINBLOCK value and the largest
MAXBLOCK values across all files, and it sums the values of #BLOCKS,
LENGTH-ERRORS, and DATA-ERRORS for all the files. The summary also reports

8. FILES, the number of pairs of files compared.

EXAMPLE

The PROC TAPECOMP step shown below compares three files on two tapes
mounted on drives 181 and 182. The tapes are forward-spaced two tapemarks.
CP DETACH commands are issued automatically after the comparisons complete.
The results of the comparisons are shown in **Output A5.1**.

```
PROC TAPECOMP TAP1 TAP2 FSF=2 MAXFILES=3 DETACHALL;
```

Output A5.1   Sample TAPECOMP Output Comparing Three Files

```
                                           SAS


                     INDIVIDUAL FILE REPORT
           ❶                                    ❶

DENSITY OF TAP1: 1600                   DENSITY OF TAP2: 1600
           ❷        ❸        ❹        ❺        ❻        ❼

DEVICE     FILENO MINBLOCK MAXBLOCK #BLOCKS LENGTH-ERRORS DATA-ERRORS

TAP1          3      87      3285      3

TAP2          3      87       785      3          1           42


                     INDIVIDUAL FILE REPORT


DENSITY OF TAP1: 1600                   DENSITY OF TAP2: 1600


DEVICE     FILENO MINBLOCK MAXBLOCK #BLOCKS LENGTH-ERRORS DATA-ERRORS

TAP1          4      87       193      3

TAP2          4      87       205      3          2           26


                     INDIVIDUAL FILE REPORT


DENSITY OF TAP1: 1600                   DENSITY OF TAP2: 1600


DEVICE     FILENO MINBLOCK MAXBLOCK #BLOCKS LENGTH-ERRORS DATA-ERRORS

TAP1          5     389      4101      4

TAP2          5      87      3073      4          4            0

_____


                     SUMMARY REPORT
```

```
                                           SAS
           ❽

DEVICE     FILES MINBLOCK MAXBLOCK #BLOCKS LENGTH-ERRORS DATA-ERRORS



TAP1          3      87      4101     10

TAP2          3      87      3073     10          7           68
```

Index

Proofreading is performed in the **Technical Writing Department** by **Frances A. Kienzle, E. Ellen Fussell, Mariam C. Chilman**, and **David A. Teal** under the supervision of **David D. Baggett**. **Gigi Hassan** is index editor. **Lisa K. Hunt** and **Drew T. Saunders** provide text entry support.

Graphic Arts provides coding, typesetting and production under the direction of **Carol M. Thompson**. For this book preliminary production was provided by **Gail C. Freeman**. Final production was provided by **Joseph H. Moore, Jr**. Text composition programming was provided by **Craig R. Sampson, Pamela A. Troutman**, and **Cynthia M. Hopkins**.

Creative Services artist **Lisa N. Clements** provided illustrations under the direction of **Jennifer A. Davis**.

Your Turn

If you have comments about SAS software or the *SAS Companion for the CMS Operating System, 1986 Edition*, please send us your ideas on a photocopy of this page. If you include your name and address, we will reply to you.

Please return to the Publications Division, SAS Institute Inc., SAS Circle, Box 8000, Cary, NC 27512-8000.